Writers' Choices

Where Learning Comes to Life

TECHNOLOGY

Technology is changing the learning experience, by increasing the power of your textbook and other learning materials; by allowing you to access more information, more quickly; and by bringing a wider array of choices in your course and content information sources.

Harcourt College Publishers has developed the most comprehensive Web sites, e-books, and electronic learning materials on the market to help you use technology to achieve your goals.

PARTNERS IN LEARNING

Harcourt partners with other companies to make technology work for you and to supply the learning resources you want and need. More importantly, Harcourt and its partners provide avenues to help you reduce your research time of numerous information sources.

Harcourt College Publishers and its partners offer increased opportunities to enhance your learning resources and address your learning style. With quick access to chapter-specific Web sites and e-books . . . from interactive study materials to quizzing, testing, and career advice . . . Harcourt and its partners bring learning to life.

Harcourt's partnership with Digital:Convergence™ brings :CRQ™ technology and the :CueCat™ reader to you and allows Harcourt to provide you with a complete and dynamic list of resources designed to help you achieve your learning goals. You can download the free :CRQ software from www.crq.com. Visit any of the 7,100 RadioShack stores nationwide to obtain a free :CueCat reader. Just swipe the cue with the :CueCat reader to view a list of Harcourt's partners and Harcourt's print and electronic learning solutions.

http://www.harcourtcollege.com/partners

Writers' Choices

Grammar to Improve Style

Michael Kischner
North Seattle Community College

Edith Wollin
North Seattle Community College

Harcourt College Publishers

Fort Worth Philadelphia San Diego New York Orlando Austin San Antonio
Toronto Montreal London Sydney Tokyo

Publisher	Earl McPeek
Acquisitions Editor	Julie McBurney
Marketing Strategist	John Meyers
Project Manager	Andrea Archer

Cover design: John Ritland / Ritland Publishing Services

ISBN: 0-15-506374-X
Library of Congress Catalog Card Number: 2001090672

Address for Domestic Orders
Harcourt College Publishers, 6277 Sea Harbor Drive, Orlando, FL 32887-6777
800-782-4479

Address for International Orders
International Customer Service
Harcourt College Publishers, 6277 Sea Harbor Drive, Orlando, FL 32887-6777
407-345-3800
(fax) 407-345-4060
(email) hbintl@harcourt.com

Address for Editorial Correspondence
Harcourt College Publishers, 301 Commerce Street, Suite 3700, Fort Worth, TX 76102

Web Site Address
http://www.harcourtcollege.com

Printed in the United States of America

0 1 2 3 4 5 6 7 8 9 039 9 8 7 6 5 4 3 2 1

Harcourt College Publishers

Brief Contents

Detailed Contents

To the Instructor

We wrote this book partly for our fellow college writing teachers who have wished there were an effective and efficient way to teach sentence structure and style while still giving adequate time to the writing process, critical reading, and the other important concerns of college composition. Such teachers typically find that it is impossible to teach grammar quickly. There are so many building blocks to put in place that we often give up in favor of an ad hoc approach—a lesson on clauses to curb the spread of fragments, a drill on restrictive and nonrestrictive elements to arrest comma delinquency, and so forth. Associated in the students' minds with the errors that prompted them and disconnected from any comprehensible whole, these units are seldom a memorable part of the course.

We believe this book can help change that. It approaches English syntax as something to delight in and experiment with. Focusing not on what students cannot do but rather on the many things they can do with sentence structures, it helps turn unconscious practice into conscious knowledge and then solidifies the knowledge by having the students put it into immediate conscious practice. The book does not say, "Avoid this—it makes your writing bad." It says, "Try this—it can make your writing strong."

We do not pretend that it is possible to teach grammar quickly. We do believe that with brief, focused explanations supported by many examples, followed by the direct application of what they learn, students can grasp a thorough overview of the phrases and clauses from which English sentences are built. We also see an important role for the instructor in this learning, from choosing the order of chapters to be studied to determining how much supplemental explanation of the material might suit a particular group of students.

We have arranged our chapters in one logical order. The first two chapters introduce students to some basic terms and concepts they encounter in the rest of the book. Most of these come from traditional syntax, with some coming from phrase structure grammar. Brief exercises in the chapters help students check their comprehension of each section. We do not, however, expect students unfamiliar with grammar terminology to learn it all from these introductory chapters. When the terms come up again in later chapters of the book, instructors may need to refresh students' memories of their meanings and to remind them that the glossary at the back of the book includes explanations of terms with which the students may be unfamiliar.

Much of the time, even when their memory of the meaning of a term is hazy, students will be able to understand what the chapter is teaching. Indeed, for the attentive student, the book can largely teach itself (which makes it useful for distance learning).

The core of the book, chapters 3–13, starts with chapters on appositive nouns and appositive adjectives. These structures are both fairly easy to learn and stylistically quite useful, so students will quickly gain a sense of mastering and applying practical knowledge. The next three chapters cover dependent clauses; these are followed by four chapters on verbal phrases, many of which can be seen as reductions of dependent clauses. We end with a chapter that recapitulates a topic touched on in each chapter, coordination and parallelism.

Some instructors may prefer to group together the chapters dealing with, say, nominal structures (appositives, noun clauses, gerund phrases, certain infinitives) and then to move on to modifying structures (relative clauses, participle phrases, infinitive phrases). Others may have a different plan. Because the chapters are largely self-contained, the book permits this. The organization of the core chapters (3–13) will become familiar, leaving room for individual instructors to emphasize different aspects of the material. Each core chapter has the following section headings.

What [the Structures] Look Like

The examples that open each chapter are important. In them, we try to illustrate most of the forms and syntactic functions of the given structure. The number of examples varies from chapter to chapter because some structures have more variations than others. There are many more variations of the relative clause, for instance, than there are of the gerund phrase. We hope instructors will help students observe the similarities and differences in each set of opening examples.

How Grammarians Describe [the Structures]

In this section we teach what we think the student needs to understand about a structure in order to use it correctly and effectively. We have tried to be accurate, not comprehensive. In discussing participle phrases, we concentrate on the common present and past participle forms, leaving it to instructors to decide whether to get into the rarer perfect and passive forms (*having been promoted*). In the chapter on appositive adjectives, we do not point out that only adjectives that can complement linking verbs can be appositive. We trust that, especially among native speakers, it is the rare student who might be tempted to write *The fool, utter and complete, dominated the conversation.* However, instructors with many ESL students may want to cover this point.

How [the Structures] Are Punctuated

We concentrate here on how punctuation follows syntax rather than on a list of simple dos and don'ts; the word "usually" appears more often than the more comforting "always." Although we have tried to supply helpful examples, instructors may wish to elaborate on some of the more grammar-based explanations. Just before the sentence-combining exercises, we have supplied a box with a summary of the basic punctuation rules for the structure in question for students to refer to as they do the exercises. Appendix A, "Common Surface Problems," addresses the most common punctuation errors and how to fix them.

What You Can Do with [the Structures]

Our goal is to expand the student writer's repertoire of conscious syntactic choices. This section considers some of the stylistic effects of those choices. Here most of the subtopics vary from chapter to chapter. When considering adverb clauses, we show how they can be used to show relations among ideas and to vary sentence length and rhythm; when considering participle phrases, we examine their ability to tighten the focus of a paragraph and to add verb power in adjective slots. We have purposely abbreviated our commentary on these subtopics in the belief that explications of style are usually more fascinating to the explicator than they are to the reader. Often this has meant reining in our own enthusiasm. We hope instructors in the classroom will give free rein to theirs as they add their own observations and examples.

Exercises

Roughly half of each chapter is composed of exercises. We supply the answers for most of them (see answer key), but instructors can do much to clarify the possible choices so that students get the most benefit from the exercises. All the chapters have the following exercises (some have additional exercises).

Practicing Sentence Combining

Writing Your Own [Structure]

[Structure] in Published Writing

Combining in Context

Revising Your Writing for Style

The twenty exercises in the "Practicing Sentence Combining" sections use semi-open combining: We name the structure that the student is to use, and we sometimes specify which base sentence or subordinator to use. Still, there is sometimes room for variation in the answers, and even more room for group discussion of these variations. Instructors should remind students regularly that sentences appear within larger blocks of discourse and that context will often determine the best form for a sentence to take.

The instructor's main role in the sentence combining exercises, however, is to make sure that the exercises are done regularly and thoroughly. We put twenty of them in each chapter because it is important to expose students to a pattern over and over again; it is from repeated exposure that the brain hypothesizes rules and picks up a syntactic pattern. This is central to the methodology of the book. Our own experience with sentence combining has amply supported the conclusions of Daiker, Kerek, and Morenberg in their extensive research: "Sentence combining clearly helps accelerate syntactic growth, even among young adults, and it is significantly more effective than the conventional essay-analysis approach in increasing the overall writing skills of college freshmen."[1]

Once the students have a clear grasp of a pattern, they can use it in the next exercise section, "Writing Your Own [Structure]" to create their own sentences. Although students may feel as though they are investing a lot of time and energy in mastering a single pattern, instructors can remind them of the final goal, which is to master many patterns and, with such mastery, to gain both a conscious and unconscious sense of the innumerable ways that something can be said in English.

---

[1] From Donald A. Daiker, Andrew Kerek, and Max Morenberg, "The Effects of Intensive Sentence Combining on the Writing Ability of College Freshmen," in Donald McQuade, ed., *Linguistics, Stylistics, and the Teaching of Composition* (New York: CUNY, 1979), 84.

After the students have mastered the pattern in individual sentences, the exercises shift to using the pattern to create better paragraphs. In "[Structure] in Published Writing" we print a passage by a published writer and ask students to locate and comment on the use of a certain structure in the passage. We ask them to think of other possible phrasings for the same information and then to compare the effects of these phrasings with the effects of the original. The answer key reproduces the passage with the relevant structures in boldface, but discussion of variant phrasings and stylistic effects are left to the students and their instructors.

After seeing the structure at work in a block of professionally written text, the students have an opportunity in "Combining in Context" to use the structure in revising two paragraphs. We have labored hard over these to make them varied in subject matter and appropriate for college-level writing. We understand that students may find the exercises laborious and hope that instructors will find at least one in each chapter to wax enthusiastic about.

The "Combining in Context" exercises are, among other things, excellent preparation for the final exercise, "Revising Your Writing for Style," which asks students to revise a piece of their own writing using the specified structure where effective. If this book is used as a supplement in a composition course, the students' own writing should be readily available. Instructors may ask students to revise paragraphs in an essay they have already written.

Instructors who do not use a handbook—as well as those who do!—may find appendix A, "Common Surface Problems," useful in marking student essays. In an informal survey in one composition class at the University of Washington, students who compared this section with similar sections in three popular handbooks found ours the most user-friendly. It first lists twenty-five problems and correction symbols to use for them. Then it gives a brief explanation of each problem and an example of how to fix it. For our list, we relied both on published research by Connors and Lunsford[2] and on our many years of experience as writing teachers. We grouped the twenty-five items under fourteen headings in an order that should allow students to find them quickly—first, those indicated by punctuation symbols; and then, those indicated by abbreviations, in alphabetical order.

---

[2] Robert J. Connors and Andrea A. Lunsford, "Frequency of Formal Errors in Current College Writing, or Ma and Pa Kettle Do Research," *College Composition and Communication,* vol. 39 (1988), 395–409.

Textbooks on style are often replete with jewels from the prose masters. We have deliberately displayed only a few such jewels. Our first concern has been to convince students that what we teach here—correct and effective use of a range of syntactic structures—is entirely within their ken. Rather than asking them to gaze upon the lapidary triumphs of Virginia Woolf or James Baldwin, we want them to look at well-shaped sentences that they themselves could have written and then to write their own. We have gazed admiringly on many sentences created by our students, not so much because the sentences were brilliant—although they sometimes were—but because they represented exciting steps beyond structures the students had attempted before. Each such step expanded the students' freedom of choice in self-expression. As we remind the students elsewhere, such freedom brings power and pleasure. We hope our book helps you and your students to experience much of both.

To the Student

This book will strengthen your knowledge of English sentence structure and show you how to apply this knowledge to your writing. Its goal is to expand your range of choice among the many ways of expressing an idea. For instance, here are four ways of expressing the same idea.

- Michael Jordan retired, and the Chicago Bulls went downhill.
- After Michael Jordan retired, the Chicago Bulls went downhill.
- The Chicago Bulls went downhill after Michael Jordan retired.
- With Michael Jordan gone, the Chicago Bulls went downhill.

Practiced writers delight in such choices. They know that each choice results in a slightly different emphasis, rhythm, or effect; they also know that one sentence may fit better than another with the sentences that come before and after it in a paragraph. They are like painters who know that the primary colors on their palette can be combined into hundreds of different shades from which they can choose just the right ones for a particular purpose.

One powerful theory maintains that sentences, too, result from combinations—performed by the incredible language computers we all have in our brains. Since you began to speak, your mental language computer has produced an astonishing number of intricate word and sentence combinations.

Most people who use real computers admit that they use only a fraction of their computers' capabilities. Many of us learn just the basic operations we need for our own purposes, feeling we lack the time or the competence to explore the options hidden inside menus with scary headings such as "Format" and "Preferences." Sometimes a helpful person comes along and shows us that the menus contain some simple operation that, had we known about it earlier, could have saved us a lot of time and trouble. Try composing a two-column list on a word processor without knowing how to insert a table, for instance.

This book is about some of the language operations your mental language computer can perform that you may not be conscious of. The system for describing these operations is called grammar, and it uses terms that are even scarier to most people than computer terms. The branch of grammar dealing specifically with sentence structure is called syntax. In syntax we find such terms as compound sentence, adverb clause, and nominative absolute. The first sentence about Michael Jordan in the example is a compound sentence; the second and third contain an adverb clause; the fourth contains a nominative absolute.

In this book, we show you that these are names of language operations that are rather easy to learn and very useful to know. Most of them you use already. Going through this book will give you a more conscious understanding of when, how, and why to use them. Practicing them will make them more available in your menu of options to use in your writing.

After an introductory chapter reviewing the basics of English syntax, the chapters of this book discuss, one at a time, some of the sentence structures that successful writers find most useful. These are treated briefly and clearly under the following headings: "What [the Structures] Look Like," "How Grammarians Describe [the Structures]," "How [the Structures] Are Punctuated," and "What You Can Do with [the Structures]." Exercises then give you practice in using the structures, first to combine and revise sentences and then to create your own sentences. Further exercises enable you to work on sentences within the larger contexts of paragraphs and finally on sentences in your own essays.

This, then, is a book about what you can do, not what you cannot do. You will find little here about errors. Instead, you will find a lot about structures and strategies that can make your writing strong, clear, and varied. In the course of practicing these structures, you will create scores of correct, effective sentences. We think this is a lot more useful than fixing incorrect sentences, and it certainly gives more pleasure. It is the kind of pleasure that successful writers enjoy as they explore the possibilities of language, and we hope such pleasure will continue to be yours long after you are finished with this book.

Chapter 1

A Few Things to Get Started

We believe that with a little grammar and a lot of practice combining sentences, you can become a much better writer. Practicing techniques for combining sentences will give you choices about how to say what you want to say. We have kept the grammar to a minimum, but it is there, and you are going to have to know a few things in order to follow the book.

Grammar

People often use "grammar" to mean the conventions of correct language use, that is, social decisions about what is right and wrong. These conventions make it seem better to say *John isn't* instead of *John ain't, John likes* instead of *John like, everyone is* instead of *everyone are,* and *themselves* instead of *theirselves.* The focus of this book is not on these conventions; we point to them only in passing.

For us, grammar is the study of the rules that govern a language as they are deduced by analyzing the language. Because these rules for language are created by the structuring of the brain and because we do not yet fully understand the brain's language-structuring system, we must rely on deduction to figure out what is happening in a language. People don't make up the grammar of a language; they look at the language and try to describe it. For that reason, not everyone agrees on all points of the description. You will notice that at various places in this book, we tell you that there is not complete agreement on how to describe something that happens in English.

Grammar covers morphology, which looks at the form and structure of words; phonology, which looks at the sound system of a language; semantics, which looks at the meanings of words and word groups; and finally syntax, which looks at the arrangement of words into phrases and sentences. The syntax of English is the focus of this book.

SYNTAX

Syntax is one part of the study of grammar. Syntax deals with the **phrases** (see Phrases section of this chapter) that make up a sentence and with the word order in those phrases and in the sentence as a whole. For instance, in English we say *the red balloon* rather than *the balloon red,* which the French would say—except with French words, *le ballon rouge.* In English we also say *John likes to fish,* not ∅*Likes John to fish.**

PARTS OF SPEECH: FORM AND FUNCTION

The parts of speech, which might be called the parts of language, are the classes of words that fit into the syntax of the sentence. You are probably familiar with the names of at least four important classes: **nouns, verbs, adjectives,** and **adverbs.** Other parts of speech include **pronouns, determiners, prepositions,** and **conjunctions.** Appendix B includes a full chart of the parts of speech with examples.

---

*The ∅ sign before a sentence signals that it is grammatically unacceptable to a native speaker.

The traditional definitions of the parts of speech tend to classify words in terms of meaning: nouns name persons, places, or things; verbs show action or state of being. Although there is some truth to these definitions, modern grammarians find that form and function are more accurate guides to which part of speech a word falls into. **Form** refers to the outer shape of words, mainly how they are pronounced and spelled. For instance, a noun such as *acrobat* takes an *-s* to form the plural, *acrobats;* this is an aspect of its form. **Function** refers to what words can do in sentences and where they are placed in relation to other words. For instance, *acrobat* can follow *the* or *an* to form a grammatical unit in a sentence (*the acrobat*), and it can be the **subject** (see Subjects and Verbs section of this chapter) of a **verb** such as *arrived* (*The acrobat arrived.*); these are aspects of its function. We can spot *arrived* as a verb partly by the *-ed* ending, which is an aspect of its form; and partly by its combining with the subject *acrobat* to make a statement about it (some grammarians call this a predication), which is an aspect of its function. In the next chapter, we look at the form and function of adjectives and adverbs.

Of course, many words fall into more than one part of speech. It is only when we see them in sentences that we can look at the function as well as form to see how they are being used. Is *jog* a verb or a noun? Depending on the sentence, it can be either.

Serena **jogged** to the university all year.
It is quite a **jog**.

In the first sentence the *-ed* in *jogged* and its joining with *Serena* to make a statement about *Serena* (*Serena jogged.*) tells us that *jogged* is a verb; in the second sentence, the *a* immediately before *jog* tells us that it is a noun.

Try these: Look at form and function to determine whether the italicized word in each pair of sentences is a noun or a verb.

1. Sandy's *book* was published last month. She has *booked* tickets for a national tour.
2. I *met* with my last boss every month. I *meet* with my present boss every day.
3. There are many *theories* about whale songs. One *theory* is that they are mating calls.
4. Scientists have *mapped* the human genome. At this point, the *maps* are still crude.
5. Your last *fax* didn't come through. *Fax* it again.

PHRASES

Phrases are groups of words that function as units within a sentence. A phrase usually has a headword and other words that associate with that headword according to grammatical rules. A **noun phrase** includes a noun headword and the words that associate with the noun headword; a **verb phrase** contains a verb headword and the words that associate with it; a **prepositional phrase** begins with a preposition and ends with a noun phrase. You will notice in the examples that follow that noun and verb phrases can contain other phrases—for instance prepositional phrases—within them. Much of this book focuses on writing phrases that will help give you choices about the way you construct sentences.

Noun Phrases

the tabby cat

the ripe banana

a bunch of grapes

Verb Phrases

hit the ball over the fence

walked to the store

cried frequently during the night

Prepositional Phrases

of grapes

over the fence

during the night

SUBJECTS AND VERBS

You need to be able to find a subject and verb in a sentence. This is not hard to do, and with a little practice, you will be proficient. Often it is easier to find the verb first; it is the word or words that need to be changed in some way to change the time of the sentence. For instance, in *Mildred drinks carrot juice, drinks* needs to be changed to *drank* if this happened in the past: *Mildred drank carrot juice (yesterday).* In various textbooks, you might find the verb called by other names, including finite verb, predicating verb, or simple predicate. In this book, we refer to it as the verb.

You have probably noticed that the verb often consists of more than one word, the **base verb,** also called the **main verb,** which carries the dictionary meaning of the verb, and **helping verbs** or **auxiliary verbs,** which help indicate time (tense) and whether an action is in a state of completeness or is still in progress (aspect).

> Jorge **returned** to the United States from Spain.
> John **is flying** to the Tulip Festival in Holland this year.
> The stolen diamond **has** never **been returned.**

In these sentences, it is the auxiliary verb that changes to show a change in the time of the sentence—*returned* changes to *returns* or *will return; is flying* changes to *was flying* or *will be flying; has been returned* to *had been returned.*

Once you have found the verb, the **subject** is the word that the verb is talking about. Who returned? *Jorge.* Who is flying? *John.* What has never been returned? *The stolen diamond.* In statements, the subject is the noun or noun substitute that normally comes before the verb. In questions, the subject comes after the verb or part of the verb.

> Is the **toast** ready?
> Did **Jorge** return to the United States from Spain?

Try these: Identify the subject and verb in the following sentences.

1. The child reached U.S. shores alone.
2. Did you see the Beatles in a live concert?
3. Where were you during the storm?
4. The package has arrived safely.
5. A dog did not dig that hole.

Sentences

A sentence is made up of two parts, a complete subject and a predicate. The **complete subject** includes the subject and the words associated with it; the **predicate** includes the verb and the words associated with it. Notice that the subject is made up of a noun phrase; the predicate is made up of a verb phrase and may also include a noun phrase.

Complete Subject	Predicate
My Aunt Ellen	works in a lawyer's office.
Sunset	is very late in northern latitudes at midsummer.
Students in the art class	drew sketches of the models posing for them.

Try these: Identify the complete subjects and predicates in the following sentences.

1. Mary Lou picked only the yellow flowers for the bouquet.
2. The red fire engine honked loudly at the intersection.
3. Ten of the children have had their measles shot already.
4. Physics is a hard but rewarding study.
5. Evolutionary biology is used to study human psychology.

Sentence Patterns

There are five to ten basic patterns that an English sentence can have; grammarians and linguists are not in complete agreement on the number. All the patterns have a subject and a verb. Others have **direct objects, indirect objects, subject complements,** and **object complements.** We are not going to go into these patterns in any detail. However, you will have a better chance of using the structures of English to your advantage if you recognize a few basic elements of some patterns—elements such as a direct object and a subject complement. (For a look at the basic patterns, see the Basic Sentence Patterns chart in appendix C.)

Sentence patterns are determined by the type of verb in the sentence—intransitive, transitive, and linking. **Intransitive verbs,** which are frequently verbs of motion, do not need a **complement**—that is, a completer such as a direct object or a subject complement—to be complete, to feel finished. The sentences do often include modifiers, a topic that we cover in the next chapter, but no other words are absolutely necessary to finish the predicate part of the sentence. Examples of intransitive verbs are *come, go, walk, run,* and *arrive.*

Complete Subject	Predicate (intransitive verb)
Tuan	walks (everyday).
Alex	came home (last night).
Nadine	sleeps (well).

Transitive verbs do need a complement; they need a direct object to finish the predicate. These **direct objects** are nouns or noun substitutes. We often say that the direct object receives the action of the verb. Common transitive verbs are *bake, hit, answer, ask, cut, set,* and *lay.*

Complete Subject	Predicate (transitive verb + complement)
Julian	**baked** *a cake* for his sister's birthday.
The students	**answered** *the questions* quickly and easily.

The *cake* is what Julian baked; *the questions* are what the students answered.

Try these: Find the subject, verb, and direct object in the following sentences.

1. The pastry chef stirred the ganache.
2. The westerly winds whipped the ocean into white foam.
3. The ice cooled her forehead.
4. The eager student interrupted the teacher with a question.
5. Shakespeare wrote tragedies in his youth.

Linking verbs also need a complement to complete their predication; they act like an equal sign between the subject and the noun or adjective that comes after them. This noun or adjective either renames or modifies the subject; the noun or adjective after a linking verb is called a **subject complement.** Common linking verbs are *be* (*am, are, is, was, were*), *seem, become,* and *appear.*

Complete Subject	Predicate (linking verb + complement)
Adrian	**seemed** *happy* with his present.
The chief of police	**was** an honest *man.*

In these examples *happy* is a subject complement describing Adrian, and *man* is a subject complement renaming the chief of police.

Try these: Find the subjects, verbs, and subject complements in the following sentences.

1. Lucy was lucky.
2. The crowd seemed angry about the delay.
3. His suit was the color of oranges.
4. That is weirdness.
5. During the fifth act of *Hamlet,* Alice became sleepy.

Depending on their use, some verbs can function in two categories or even in all three categories, but when they do, their meaning varies somewhat from category to category.

COMPLETE SUBJECT	PREDICATE
Tuan	**walked** to the store. (intransitive)
Tuan	**walked** his *dog* after dinner. (transitive)
Jane	**turned** the *page.* (transitive)
The *leaves*	**turned** bright *red* in the chilly, dry autumn nights. (linking)
The *bamboo*	**grew** rapidly. (intransitive)
The retired *man*	**grew** prize winning *roses.* (transitive)
The *audience*	**grew** *restless* during the long intermission. (linking)

INDEPENDENT AND DEPENDENT CLAUSES

An **independent clause** has a basic sentence pattern, so it must at least have a subject and predicate, and it can stand alone as a sentence. The following are all independent clauses; find the subjects and verbs in them.

Norton rocked the cradle.
The NRA does not support gun control.
At the family picnic, the teenagers wandered off by themselves.
Neurons were visible to the naked eye.

A **dependent clause** also has a basic sentence pattern, so it too has a subject and verb; however, dependent clauses are preceded by words (sometimes implied words) that keep them from being able to stand alone as sentences. We look more closely at those words and the structures they create later in the book. For now, here are some dependent clauses.

> While the wind roared
> When Mt. Rainier erupts
> who wears a red sweater
> that I have ever seen

These dependent clauses must be attached to an independent clause in order to make a sentence. If *who wears a red sweater* were followed by a question mark, it would be independent and could stand alone; without a question mark, it is a dependent clause.

Try these: Identify the independent and dependent clauses in the following sentences.

1. Nell swam to shore after her canoe capsized.
2. Einstein is the person who recognized time as a fourth dimension.
3. While the war raged, the scientists at Los Alamos worked in their labs.
4. When the Chinook winds sweep down the mountains, the snow melts.
5. When the bases are loaded, you want the next batter to be good.

Fragments

Dependent clauses and phrases, when they are not attached to an independent clause, are called sentence fragments or fragments. In fact any structure that does not contain an independent clause is a fragment.

> Running out of water.
> In a train to Miami.
> After the ski trip was over.

Often in spoken language we communicate in fragments—in fact, the closer we are to someone, the more fragments we use to communicate. We answer questions with *yeah, OK, clearly,* and *because I was late;* we ask questions with *now? today? really?* and *want to leave now?*

Even in written English, fragments can sometimes be effective. However, they usually are not effective, and, worse, they are often confusing. If you punctuate a dependent clause or a phrase as if it were an independent clause (a sentence), you risk confusing your reader. Even the grammar check on your word processor gets upset about fragments! However, we have discovered that our word processor's grammar check thinks that some things that are not fragments are and vice versa, so do not trust your word processor to take care of this problem for you; for instance, ours does not recognize *The stolen diamond.* as a fragment.

Try these: Which of the following are fragments?

1. When DNS was discovered.
2. Yoga is commonly suggested as a stress reliever.
3. Leaning into the wind.
4. During the sociology class.
5. Mothers know when their children need them.

BASE SENTENCES

The **base sentence** is the independent clause; it is also called the **main clause.** The aim of this book is to show how to attach syntactic structures to the base sentence; some of them, such as adjectives and prepositional phrases, will become part of the base sentence; others, such as dependent clauses, do not.

ACTIVE AND PASSIVE VOICE

Only the transitive verbs, the verbs that take a direct object, have voice. In **active voice,** the subject does the action of the verb and the direct object receives the action of the verb.

The *mime* **imitated** the *politician.*

In **passive voice,** the word that was the direct object of the sentence becomes the subject.

The *politician* ***was*** **imitated** (*by the mime*).

Notice that although the word that was the subject in the active voice sentence can appear in a prepositional phrase beginning with *by* or *for,* it may not be present in the passive voice sentence at all. And there is also a change in the verb; a form of *be* is added to the base verb (*was* in the example sentence) and the base verb takes the past participle form. For regular verbs, the past participle ends in *-ed;* there is no difference between the forms of the past tense and the past participle (*imitated* in the example sentence).

Ariana **bakes** a cake every Sunday.
A cake **is baked** (by Ariana) every Sunday.

Yahweh **made** a human from the earth.
A human **was made** from the earth (by Yahweh).

Diyin DinÇale **created** the fifth world.
The fifth world **was created** (by Diyin DinÇale).

Men **break** my heart.
My heart **is broken** (by men).

A lot of composition teachers and the grammar check on your word processor will tell you that you should not use the passive voice. As with most absolute rules, this one should be broken when there is good reason to break it. Of course, you should avoid using passive voice if it creates wordy, unfocused sentences or suggests that the subject is receiving the action when you really want to focus on the subject as the actor. It takes a reader longer to comprehend passive voice sentences, so you want to use them with discretion.

However, there are times when you do want to stress that the subject is receiving the action. When a window is broken during a storm or an earthquake, we usually want to emphasize that the window was broken, not that the storm or the earthquake did the action. In fact, it sounds a bit bizarre to say, *The earthquake broke the window.* We also use the passive when we really do not know who did the action. The window may be broken, but we may have no idea who broke it, so we use the passive voice structure without the *by* prepositional phrase. We also use the passive when a vague someone does the action. For example, someone does make shirts in a manufacturing plant in Mexico, but it sounds strange in English to say, *Someone made this shirt in Mexico.* Instead, we use the passive.

This shirt **was made** in Mexico.

We can also use the passive within a paragraph to help paragraph coherence. Usually the beginning of a sentence contains information that repeats or is linked to information in the previous sentence or sentences. Using passive voice can make this kind of link possible.

Nerve gas killed twelve people and injured 5,500 in a Tokyo subway.
The gas **was set off** by members of the Aum Shinri Kyo religious sect.

Notice how much better the paragraph coherence works with the passive than it does in the following version with the second sentence in active voice.

> Nerve gas killed twelve people and injured 5,500 in a Tokyo subway. Members of the Aum Shinri Kyo religious sect **set off** the gas.

One common use of the passive voice is really a misuse of the passive. Because the *by* prepositional phrase that contains the doer of the action can be omitted in the passive, it is possible to omit the person or group responsible for an action or a decision even when the doer is known. So governments and businesses will frequently report that *a decision was made.* There is a pretense in this use of passive voice that no one is responsible for this decision, one that might involve loss of jobs or even deaths. Because this kind of lie is recognized by good critical readers, its effectiveness as a rhetorical device is lost. In addition, effective rhetoric should be at the service of truth, not lies.

Try these: Which of the following have verbs in the passive voice?

1. The drunk driver was arrested shortly after leaving the scene of the accident.
2. The arresting officer read him his Miranda rights.
3. Qualifying for the Olympics is a major victory.
4. Since DNA was discovered, huge advances in biology have occurred.
5. The swelling caused great pain. The pain was relieved by the cold compress.

Expletives

In grammar, an **expletive** is a word that carries no semantic meaning in a sentence but sits in the position where a word, phrase, or clause that does carry meaning would ordinarily sit. English is a word-order language—we know that a noun is the subject and not the direct object by its place in the sentence, not by an ending attached to the word. If the subject does not appear before the verb but is put in another place in the sentence, an expletive must fill the subject slot. *There* and *it* are the two most common expletives in English.

> **There** are many *reasons* to question the special prosecutor's authority.
> **It** is impossible *for the football team to win this game.*

Coordination and Parallelism

Coordination and parallelism are such important tools in writing that we illustrate them throughout the book with every structure we discuss; at the end of the book, there is a chapter reviewing the whole topic. The following definitions should be enough for now.

Coordination involves a series of two or more grammatically equal units of a sentence—words, phrases, or clauses. They are usually joined by one of seven coordinating conjunctions: *and, but, or, nor, for, yet,* and *so.*

Coordinate words:	**Moths** and **butterflies** belong to the same family.
Coordinate phrases:	Sarah sailed **through the semifinals** and **into the finals.**
Coordinate clauses:	I do not know **who did it** or **why it was done.**

Parallelism commonly refers to a series of three or more coordinate sentence units, with each unit containing more than one word that is coordinate with words in the other units.

> The celebration featured **perfect weather, splendid fireworks,** and **happy crowds.**

So there you have it—everything you ever needed to know about grammar! In this book, we also talk about punctuation as it relates to syntax. As we said at the beginning, we do not deal much with the conventions of standard usage—such as subject-verb agreement and pronoun agreement—but from time to time we mention those conventions that are relevant to something we are discussing, split infinitives and the use of *who* and *whom* for instance. Also we say very little about word choice in this book; that does not mean that we think that any word will do if you have great syntax. You still have to search, as all great writers do, for the right word. With the right words and the right syntax, the world of language is yours.

CHAPTER 2

Modification

In the preceding chapter, we reviewed the elements that every sentence must have—the subject and the predicate. We also noted that some predicates have complements, or completers. The final major function in a sentence is performed by **modifiers.** Sentences do not need modifiers to be grammatically complete, but most contain them.

In grammar, to modify a word is to add information to it. In the phrase *green apples,* the modifier *green* adds information to the noun *apples* so that it refers not to all apples but only to green ones. In the phrase *danced gracefully,* the modifier *gracefully* adds information to the verb *danced* so that it refers not only to an action but to how the action was performed. The added information in each case changes the meaning of the word as used in the sentence; hence the term *modifier.*

A modifier can be more than just one word, such as *green* or *gracefully.* Often we use structures—phrases and clauses—to add information to a word.

apples **on the tree**
apples **ripening in the sun**
apples **that have wormholes in them**

danced **with his partner**
danced **to express his joy in life**
danced **whenever he had a chance**

Each of the structures in boldface has a name—prepositional phrase, participle phrase, relative clause, and so forth—and a large portion of this book is about how they work and the creative things you can do with them. For now, just note that they modify the words next to them; this is the general pattern in a word-order language such as English. However, sometimes modifiers do not appear next to the word they modify, and sometimes you have choices about where you place them. Writers must make sure that their readers see clearly and unambiguously what modifies what in a sentence. So it is important to understand a few things about modification before we discuss the choices we can make in composing sentences.

Modifiers of Nouns: Adjectives and Adjectivals

The modifiers of nouns are typically **adjectives,** such as *green, large, bad, gorgeous,* and *digestible;* or **adjectival** structures, such as *on the tree, ripening in the sun,* and *that have wormholes in them* in the previous examples. In form, adjectives often have endings such as *-ous, -able,* and *-ish,* and they can be changed for comparison or intensification—*green, greener, greenest.* In function, they typically precede nouns (***green** apples*) or are linked to them as complements (*the apples are **green***), and they add information that commonly answers the questions "which?" "what kind of?" and "how many?"

Sometimes a noun is modified by a different kind of word. For instance, it can be modified by another noun, as in *the **pie** apple.* Here *pie,* a noun in form, is an **adjectival,** a word or structure performing the function of an adjective. Possessive nouns are usually adjectival as in *the **farmer's** apples.*

Nouns are often preceded by a subclass of adjectival modifiers called **determiners**—words such as *the* and *a/an; this, that, these,* and *those; my, your, its,* and *their; more, most, all, many,* and *few;* and the words for numbers such as *one* and *two,* and *fifth* and *sixth.* When both a determiner and an adjective precede a noun, the adjective is normally between the determiner and the noun, as in *the green apples* and *their tart flavor.* Contemporary grammarians use the term **noun phrase** for a noun plus any accompanying determiners and other modifiers it may have.

Try these: In the following sentences, (a) identify all the adjectives and adjectival modifiers, including determiners; and (b) identify the noun that each one modifies. The sentences include only single-word modifiers, no phrases or clauses. Of course, the same noun may be modified by more than one modifier.

1. The high seas began to cause grave concern among the ship's crew.
2. The gathering storm would reach them in a few minutes.
3. Whale blubber had many uses in the nineteenth century.
4. Fossil fuels were just being developed for home and industrial use.
5. Today, many people consider whales beautiful, complex creatures.

MODIFIERS OF VERBS: ADVERBS AND ADVERBIAL STRUCTURES

A **verb phrase** is made up of a verb and any complements and modifiers that have been added to it. You have read about complements in the previous chapter; here we look at modifiers. The modifiers of verbs are typically **adverbs** or adverbial structures such as those that might follow the verb. For instance, to *danced* we might add *with his partner, to express his joy in life,* and *whenever he had a chance.* (We study adverbial structures fairly closely later.) The information added by adverbs answers such questions as "how?" "when?" "where?" and "why?" "How?" adverbs usually have the *-ly* ending that marks many adverbs, for example, *gracefully, smoothly, carelessly,* and *beautifully.* "When?" adverbs include *now, then, often, seldom,* and *never.* "Where?" adverbs include *here, there,* and *everywhere.* "Why?" is often answered by adverbial structures, such as *to express his joy in life* and *because he had to.*

As with adjectives, words other than adverbs—specifically, a few nouns—can function adverbially. The short list includes *home* in *I walked **home*** (where?), and *nights* in *Bill works **nights*** (when?).

Try these: In the following sentences, (a) identify the verbs and (b) identify the adverbs modifying each verb. All the adverbs are single words, and there may be more than one modifier for each verb.

1. The liner moved slowly away as family members tearfully waved good-bye.
2. Soon the liner would be sailing in dangerous waters.
3. Enemy submarines were then stealthily patrolling the waters beyond the harbor.
4. Those who stayed home would not always be safe.
5. Crossing the ocean usually involved less risk.

Modifiers of Adjectives and Adverbs: Qualifiers

Both adjectives and adverbs can have modifiers of their own. *More, most, less,* and *least* can be used to intensify or weaken adjectives and adverbs.

a **more** versatile apple	danced **more** gracefully
the **most** delicious apple	danced **most** freely

Other words used to modify adjectives and adverbs include *quite, very, rather, too, awfully, almost,* and *fairly.*

a **quite** good apple	danced **quite** gracefully
a **very** nice day	graded **very** inconsistently

In traditional grammar, these modifiers are called adverbs, too. Some contemporary grammarians prefer to call them **qualifiers** and to reserve the term **adverb** for modifiers of verbs. This classification is easy to remember—adjectives modify nouns; adverbs modify verbs—and helps us focus on the principal functions of adjectives and adverbs. It also reminds us that most qualifiers are different in form from true adverbs.

Try these: Identify the qualifiers in the following sentences and indicate whether they modify adjectives or adverbs.

1. People with very pale skin should wear sunblock almost daily.
2. They should apply it very carefully to all exposed parts of their bodies.
3. Yesterday, it was too hot to play even a little tennis.
4. I was interested in more sedentary activities.
5. By evening, it had become quite comfortable.

PLACEMENT OF MODIFIERS

As we point out in the preceding chapter, English is a word-order language. Within each native English speaker, a mental language computer silently applies a set of intricate rules that dictate the order in which a series of modifiers must go in a phrase, for example, *the most consistently excellent pie apples in the region.* Thanks to this mental language computer, we do not have to trouble ourselves with these rules here. It is enough to take note of an important general difference between adjectives and adverbs—adjectives are fairly fixed in their placement; adverbs are fairly movable. When asked to insert the adjective *victorious* into *The team celebrated wildly,* most native speakers of English know to place it after the determiner and before the noun, *The* ***victorious*** *team celebrated wildly.* But look at all the places you could insert the adverb *gratefully* into *The hiker guzzled the water.*

Gratefully, the hiker guzzled the water.
The hiker **gratefully** guzzled the water.
The hiker guzzled the water **gratefully.**

This difference in placement applies not only to single-word adjectives and adverbs but to adjectival and adverbial structures as well. The movability of many adverbs and adverbial structures is worth noting because of its special usefulness when you are seeking different rhythms and emphases in your writing.

Try these: Each of the following sentences is preceded by a word in parentheses. Insert this word as a modifier into the sentence. Note whether there is more than one place it could go.

1. (noisily) The children came back to the classroom from recess.
2. (messy) A roommate can be very difficult to live with.
3. (surprise) Lena loves to give birthday parties.
4. (carefully) Because he did not want to disturb any evidence, the detective inspected the scene of the crime.
5. (careful) The skillful surgeon cut through fat and muscle to reach the stomach.

PREPOSITIONAL PHRASES

You can hardly say or write a sentence without a prepositional phrase in it. The sentence you just read has two (*without a prepositional phrase* and *in it*).

Prepositional phrases are everywhere in English sentences, partly because they can modify nouns, verbs, adjectives, and adverbs. More rarely, they are also found in sentence slots commonly filled by noun phrases (the subject slot, for example): ***Before breakfast*** *is my most productive writing time.*

A **prepositional phrase** consists of a preposition plus its object; the **object of the preposition** is a noun or a noun substitute, and it often has its own modifiers. Prepositions get their name (pre-position) from their almost always coming before their objects, for example, *on the tree, with his partner, over Poughkeepsie, about your very well-written essay, during Passover, as a clown, because of you,* and *according to Hoyle.* In question form and in the case of certain clauses that we look at later, a preposition's object may come before it.

A list of the common prepositions in English would number at least eighty. Here is list of just some of them—but remember that they don't really become prepositions until they take an object to form a prepositional phrase; to remind you of this, we supply a possible object in parentheses.

aboard (ship)
among (friends)
along with (his other virtues)
but [except] (John)
except (Sally)
from (whom)
in (it)
in accordance with (the law)
in regard to (my letter)
in spite of (my illness)
of (Mr. Howard's students)
before (graduation)
until (Ramadan)
without (your soothing presence)

When a prepositional phrase modifies a noun, it always comes right after the noun.

the apples **on the tree**
the tractors **in the field**
an offer **of peace**
their argument **over nothing**
one **of my best friends**

The last example in this list illustrates a common use of prepositional phrases beginning with *of* to modify words such as *one, two, several,* and *most.* In a sentence such as *One* ***of my best friends*** *sells insurance,* the grammatical subject of the verb *sells* is *One,* not *friends; friends* is the object of the preposition. The subject of a sentence is never found inside a prepositional phrase.

Because the object of a preposition is typically a noun, it can itself be modified by another adjectival prepositional phrase. This can result in a long string of prepositional phrases, which is not a problem as long as everything remains clear. Here is a string of four prepositional phrases in a sentence: *One* ***of the students in my class at the University of Illinois*** *missed the final.*

Adverbial prepositional phrases, like other adverbial structures, are often movable within a sentence; they do not need to be next to the verbs they modify. Often we find them at the very beginning of sentences, set off by a comma.

> **On Sunday afternoons,** my friend and I play chess.

They can also be at the end of sentences.

> The Soviet Union launched the world's first artificial satellite **in 1957.**

An important thing to remember about all modifiers is that they tend to modify the nearest word they can modify. Because prepositional phrases can modify both nouns and verbs, this can lead to ambiguity.

> Gary drank the liquor **in his father's house.**

Is *in his father's house* an adverbial prepositional phrase telling us where Gary drank or an adjectival prepositional phrase telling us which liquor Gary drank? If it is adverbial, a careful writer will place it away from *liquor* to make sure the reader interprets it as modifying *drank.* In this example, the only alternative is to move the prepositional phrase to the introductory position.

> **In his father's house,** Gary drank the liquor.

When prepositional phrases modify adjectives, the adjectives are usually in the subject complement position.

> My grandfather was kind **to me.**

In these instances, too, it is best to keep the prepositional phrase near the word it modifies. In the example, note how, if you move *to me* to the introductory position, you create a different meaning.

> **To me,** my grandfather was kind.

Here, *To me* could mean "in my opinion" and modify the entire rest of the sentence. This is another function of certain prepositional phrases such as *in my opinion, for me,* and *according to Jennifer.*

We use prepositional phrases almost unconsciously, and our mental language computers usually place them quite accurately. They are worth becoming conscious of, however, because they can be powerful tools as we write. Instead of saying that Michael Jordan played *equally gracefully and skillfully,* for instance, we can say that he played *with equal grace and skill,* using a prepositional phrase to avoid a mouthful of *-lys* and to focus more sharply on the two qualities of Jordan's playing. Abraham Lincoln did not call for *popularly elected, democratic, responsive government.* Rather, he called for *government of the people, by the people, and for the people,* enthroning the people at the top of three simple but immortal prepositional phrases. He did not say that we must hope such a government shall be *imperishable.* He said we must hope that it *shall not perish from the earth,* using another prepositional phrase to suggest the desolateness of a planet without such a government.

Imagine the sense of power and pleasure it must have given Lincoln to be able to use language this way. We cannot guarantee that prepositional phrases will make your writing immortal, but making conscious use of these phrases and the other structures in the remaining chapters of this book can certainly add both power and pleasure to your writing. Enjoy them.

Try these: Identify every prepositional phrase in the following sentences and indicate which word each phrase is modifying.

1. After the long hike, the children ate with gusto.
2. Pollution experts say we need stricter controls on emissions from all gasoline engines.
3. Outside the theater, eager young people waited impatiently in line for tickets.
4. The wise man on my right ate nothing and slept like a baby during the flight.
5. The songs of whales are full of beauty and variety, and they change in subtle ways over the course of a mating season.

CHAPTER 3

APPOSITIVES

WHAT APPOSITIVES LOOK LIKE

1. Arundhati Roy's first book, ***The God of Small Things,*** was published in 1997.
2. Challah, **a braided loaf of white egg bread,** is traditionally eaten on Jewish ceremonial occasions.
3. A hundred thousand people are expected at the free concert by the singer **Garth Brooks.**
4. **A passionate golfer,** Steve Jobs had a small putting green installed in his office.
5. Bernal Diaz, **author of *The Conquest of New Spain,*** entered Tenochtitlan—**today's Mexico City**—with Hernando Cortéz in November 1519.

6. Economists distinguish two broad types of markets: **product markets and factor markets.**
7. "When I was a boy, I leaned over the edge of one dam or another—**perhaps Long Lake or Little Falls or the great gray dragon known as the Grand Coulee**—and watched the ghosts of salmon rise from the water to the sky and become constellations." (Sherman Alexie, "The Toughest Indian in the World," *The New Yorker,* June 21 and 28, 1999, 96–106.)

How Grammarians Describe Appositives

Appositives are nouns or noun phrases that rename other nouns and fill the same grammatical slot in a sentence as the noun they rename. That is, if a noun is a subject, its appositive is a kind of substitute subject; if a noun is an object, its appositive is a kind of substitute object. So in the sentence

> My father, **a burglar,** worked nights.

the base noun *father* is the subject, and *burglar,* an appositive renaming *father,* is also a subject; *worked* is the verb for both of them. Unlike compound subjects, which normally name different things, appositives name the same thing as their base noun. (We deal with compound subjects in chapter 5.)

As with any noun, an appositive can have modifiers.

> Maurice Greene, **a promising runner by the age of seventeen,** became a champion runner only after moving to California to train under UCLA coach John Smith.

An appositive can also take the form of a noun clause (see chapter 7), as in the following example in which the clause in boldface is an appositive for the base noun *belief.*

> The belief **that there is intelligent life in outer space** is held by many scientists.

Appositives get their name from the Latin word meaning "to place near to." Typically they follow the word or structure they rename, but they sometimes precede those words or structures at the very beginning of sentences.

HOW APPOSITIVES ARE PUNCTUATED

Appositives are usually set off by commas. Much of the time, you will find them enclosed in a pair of commas—for instance, when they come between a noun and a verb.

> Arundhati Roy's first book, ***The God of Small Things,*** was published in 1997.

Sometimes, for emphasis or clarity, they are set off by dashes. This is often the case when they occur in a series.

> Many childhood diseases that used to kill or afflict millions of children—**whooping cough, measles, diphtheria, polio**—can remain a thing of the past if we keep up inoculation programs.

When an appositive comes before its base noun, which happens only at the beginning of a sentence, it is set off by a single comma.

> **A Guatemalan Indian with little formal education,** Rigoberta Menchu wrote a book that brought her to the attention of the world.

When an appositive is the final structure in a sentence, it may be set off by a colon.

> Sleeping under the Christmas tree was the children's present: **a tiny golden retriever puppy.**

No punctuation is used when an appositive is **restrictive**—that is, when it is necessary to identify its base noun. (In chapter 6, we deal at length with **restrictive** and **nonrestrictive** elements.) In the following sentence, for example, the appositive *Wallace Stevens* is not set off from the noun *poet* by commas because it is needed to identify which poet the writer is talking about.

> The poet **Wallace Stevens** was an executive of the Hartford Insurance Company.

WHAT YOU CAN DO WITH APPOSITIVES

1. Maintain Paragraph Flow and Focus

Appositives are particularly useful for adding to a sentence pertinent, helpful, and even necessary information that would interrupt the flow and focus of a paragraph and/or cause unhelpful repetition if it were in a separate sentence. Consider how the second sentence in this short paragraph interrupts both the flow and the focus.

> Dr. Richard D. Hansen declares that the ancient Maya may have brought ecological disaster upon themselves by razing forests. **Hansen is a professor of archeology at UCLA.** The Mayans burned forests to melt the lime from which they made stucco for their monuments.

The second sentence gives important information about Hansen's credentials, but it shifts attention away from the subject of the paragraph, the Maya. An appositive permits you to reduce the information to size and place it right next to the word to which it relates.

> Dr. Richard D. Hansen, **a professor of archeology at UCLA,** declares that the ancient Maya may have brought ecological disaster upon themselves by razing forests. The Mayans burned forests to melt the lime from which they made stucco for their monuments.

2. Increase Economy

A caution: economy is not always the most important thing in writing. Sometimes the longer way of saying something is clearer or more effective. In general, however, it is good to save words when you can, and appositives can help you do this. They often seem to function as reduced relative clauses (see chapter 6) from which the *who is* or *which is* has been eliminated.

> *Original sentence:* Linus Pauling, **who was a Nobel Prize–winning scientist,** suggested taking large regular doses of Vitamin C as an antioxidant.
>
> *Revision:* Linus Pauling, **a Nobel Prize–winning scientist,** suggests taking large regular doses of Vitamin C as an antioxidant.

An appositive at the beginning of a sentence can economically suggest a relation between one fact and another. Here an appositive replaces an adverb clause (see chapter 8).

> *Original sentence:* **Because he is a passionate golfer,** Steve Jobs had a putting green set up in his office.
>
> *Revision:* **A passionate golfer,** Steve Jobs had a putting green set up in his office.

FIGURE 3.1
Punctuating Appositives

Appositives are usually set off by commas.

Beginning of sentence: **An extrovert,** Aram loves parties.
Middle of sentence: Thomas Malthus, **the great economist,** was gloomy.
End of sentence: I just re-read Toni Morrison's masterpiece, ***Beloved.***

Dashes and a colon (use both sparingly and use colons only at the end of a sentence) can also be used.

Penguins—**a species of flightless bird like ostriches and emus**—have feathers.
Our noses led us to the source of the fragrance: **a blooming honeysuckle bush.**

Restrictive appositives are not punctuated.

The trumpeter and singer **Louis Armstrong** left a huge mark on American jazz.
Computer scientists have added a new meaning to the word **cookie.**

An appositive can also replace an independent clause in a compound sentence (see chapter 5).

Original sentence: A university education was once a privilege of the well-to-do in this country, but it is now available to most Americans.

Revision: **Once a privilege of the well-to-do in this country,** a university education is now available to most Americans.

3. Extend the Meaning of a Word in Context

In one of its most interesting uses, an appositive can go well beyond merely renaming a noun. You can use it to extend the meaning of a word, stating what you intend the word to mean in a particular context.

They had a beautiful marriage, **a union of romantic passion and intellectual compatibility.**
Valerie is that rarity, **a great talent with a small ego.**

4. Create Coordination and Parallelism

Appositives fit easily into series and into coordinate and parallel constructions.

Many factors—**global warming, El Niño, explosions in distant galaxies, even secret military experiments**—have been pointed to as possible causes of recent weather patterns.

Both a superb chef and a shrewd businessman, the owner of Labujnik Restaurant enjoyed financial success as well as critical acclaim for many years.

Now they all lie equal in their graves—**masters and slaves, kings and commoners, the conquerors and the conquered.**

Exercises

A. Practicing Sentence Combining

Combine each group of sentences into one sentence that uses at least one appositive. The starred sentence should remain the base sentence. In most cases, the appositive will rename a subject near the beginning of the sentence. Appositives may be compounded or in a series. Some may be placed either before or after the subject; try them both ways.

Example

*The only fatality of the Lewis and Clark expedition resulted from a ruptured appendix.
The only fatality of the Lewis and Clark expedition was Charles Floyd's death.

The only fatality of the Lewis and Clark expedition, Charles Floyd's death, resulted from a ruptured appendix.

1. *Art Tatum was completely blind.
   Art Tatum was one of the greatest jazz pianists of the century.
2. *In 1996, Gary Kasparov accepted the challenge of playing against IBM's Deep Blue.
   Gary Kasparov was world chess champion.
   Deep Blue is a powerful chess-playing computer program.
3. *Erwin Shrödinger thought life was governed by a "genetic code."
   "Genetic code" was a phrase he coined.
4. *Arthur wanted a house with a cool, dry cellar.
   This was because Arthur was a collector of rare wine.
5. *Michael Jordan was a master of every kind of shot.
   They included three pointers, slam dunks, free throws.
6. *The San Antonio Spurs's Tim Duncan is being called "the Air apparent."
   This is a pun suggesting he may be the next Michael "Air" Jordan.
7. *Yoga for kids is a burgeoning industry.
   Yoga for kids is an outgrowth of the latest adult trend.
8. *A walk around the block with little Chloe is a joy.
   A walk around the block with little Chloe is a voyage of discovery led by a tireless explorer.
9. *Florence is full of great sculptures of the young David.
   David was the symbol of young, upstart Florence challenging the power of Goliath Rome.
10. *New regulations will create three categories of sunburn protection.
    These are "minimal" (SPF 2 to 12), "moderate" (12 to 30), and "high" (30 and more).
11. *The Maya left pyramids and monuments that are among the wonders of the world.
    The Maya were an Amerindian people who flourished between 300 and 800 C.E.
12. *Their architectural and engineering achievements are found at several sites in Central America.
    These achievements were astonishing pyramids, palaces, and bas-relief scenes.

13. *The major sites are in northern Guatemala and southern Mexico.
The major sites are Uxmal, Uxactum, Copán, Piedras, and Tixal.
14. *The largest site may have had a population of 40,000 people.
The largest site was Tixal.
15. *One archeologist believes the Maya may have brought ecological disaster upon themselves.
The archeologist is Dr. Richard D. Hansen.
Dr. Richard D. Hansen is a professor at UCLA.
16. *Lime stucco is made by melting limestone.
Lime stucco is the material used in much Maya architecture.
17. *The melting of limestone led to the leveling of forests for firewood.
The melting of limestone is a process that requires intense heat.
18. *Dr. Hansen suggests that deforestation destroyed the seasonal swamps where the Maya had been collecting peat to fertilize their terraced agricultural gardens.
Deforestation is a major cause of soil erosion.
19. *Dr. David A. Freidel said Dr. Hansen's theory was convincing only when applied to the area of northern Guatemala where Dr. Hansen had been working.
Dr. David A. Freidel was another speaker at the conference where Dr. Hansen presented his theory.
20. *For the general collapse of Maya civilization, other causes may have been more important.
Other causes were population pressure on the agricultural system, constant warfare, changing trade routes, drought and other climactic factors, and competition among elites.

B. Writing Your Own Appositives

1. Write five sentences that use appositives in their normal position following their base noun. (Example: *Dave Oglethorpe, a professional hockey player, has scars all over his face.*)
2. Write five sentences that use appositives at the beginning of a sentence before their base noun. (Example: *A specialist on computer security, Phyllis is in great demand these days.*)

C. Appositives in Published Writing

Here is a passage by writer Diane Ackerman. Locate the appositives in the passage and comment on their use. How might the same information be conveyed without appositives? Compare the effects of other possible phrasings with the effect of the original.

> If you ask someone to draw a whale, she will probably draw a sperm whale, the bulbous-headed whale made famous in Melville's *Moby Dick,* a book that is as much a treatise on whales as it is a piece of fiction. But whales come in many shapes, sizes, and colors. There are two basic groups: the toothed whales (Odontoceti, from the Latin for "tooth" and "whale") and the baleen whales (Mysticeti, from the Latinized Greek word for "whale").
>
> Diane Ackerman, *The Moon by Whale Light and Other Adventures among Bats, Penguins, Crocodilians, and Whales* (New York: Random House, 1991), 115.

D. Combining in Context

Rewrite the following paragraphs, making effective use of appositives.

1. The origins of the Koran have been undergoing reexamination by Muslim and non-Muslim scholars around the world. The Koran is the sacred book of Islam. The traditional belief is still widely adhered to within Islam. It is that the Koran is the actual Word of God as revealed to the prophet Muhammad. According to this belief, the illiterate Muhammad received his revelations from the angel Gabriel and then reported them verbatim to family members and friends, who either memorized them or wrote them down. About fifteen years after Muhammad's death, Caliph 'Uthman became concerned over the growth of Islamic sects claiming differing versions of the Koranic scripture. Caliph 'Uthman was the third Islamic ruler to succeed Muhammad. He ordered a committee to gather the various pieces of scripture into one standard written version; all incomplete and "imperfect" collections were destroyed. Some modern scholars think this is an example of "salvation history." "Salvation history" is a story about a religion's origins invented later and projected back in time for religious purposes. These scholars think that the Koran, like the Bible, may be a compilation of oral and written traditions from many sources.

2. Mihaly Csikszentmihalyi is an authority on "flow" experiences. He is a professor of psychology at the University of Chicago. In one of his books, he describes flow experiences as moments of intense living when "what we feel, what we wish, and what we think are in harmony." The book is *Flow*. He identifies several conditions that are usually present in such experiences. One is clear goals. Another is immediate feedback. Another—perhaps most important—is balance between challenge and skills. He writes, "Flow tends to occur when a person's skills are fully involved in overcoming a challenge that is just about manageable." Some activities are highly likely to furnish flow experiences to those who engage in them. One is climbing a mountain. Another is playing a musical piece. Another is performing surgery. Finding flow in everyday life is harder but possible, according to Csikszentmihalyi. He believes people can take conscious steps to find flow both at work and at home and that doing so could significantly improve the lives of many people. He is an energetic optimist.

E. Revising Your Writing for Style

Choose a piece of your own writing and look for places where appositives might be used to improve the focus and flow of a paragraph or to achieve desirable economy. (Remember, not all economy is desirable!) As you revise, consider the following questions.

1. Is there information interrupting the flow and focus of your paragraphs that would fit into an appositive?
2. Are there relative clauses beginning with *who is* and *which is* that you could turn into appositives, thereby eliminating those words?

CHAPTER 4

Appositive Adjectives

What Appositive Adjectives Look Like

1. The new teacher, **young** and **inexperienced,** had trouble controlling the class.
2. Nick's room, **messy** beyond belief, was a reverse mirror of his orderly mind.
3. "Each of these three essays, **brilliant, original** and sometimes **perplexing,** deserves a review of its own. . . ." (Tamar Jacoby, review of *Rituals of Blood: Consequences of Slavery in Two American Centuries,* by Orlando Patterson, *The Washington Post Book World,* January 24, 1999, 10.)
4. **Plump, firm,** and dark **red,** the Bing cherries were at their peak of goodness.
5. "**Jaded, numbed,** and **dehumanized,** viewers and readers seem to need ever more visceral doses of violence to jump-start their emotions and sensibilities." (Michael Cart, *From Romance to Realism: 50 Years of*

Growth and Change in Young Adult Literature, New York: HarperCollins, 1996, 144.)

6. "At once **empathetic** and deeply **distressed,** Patterson writes with the angry passion of a biblical prophet. . . ." (Tamar Jacoby, [review of Orlando Patterson, *Rituals of Blood: Consequences of Slavery in Two American Centuries*], *The Washington Post Book World,* January 24, 1999, 10.)

How Grammarians Describe Appositive Adjectives

Appositive adjectives are adjectives that are placed and punctuated so that they receive a different focus in a noun phrase from that of regular adjectives. Now let us examine this rather abstract definition.

A noun phrase consists of a noun and any modifiers it may have, including determiners such as *the.* In the following sentence, the first noun phrase is italicized and its words labeled.

*The **cute little** house* on the corner has been sold.
det. adj. adj. noun

In this sentence, the adjectives, in boldface, are placed in normal English word order: they come after the determiner *the* and just before the noun *house.* No punctuation separates them from the noun. They perform the common adjectival function of adding information about the house, and in this case the information seems to help identify the particular house. This is a sentence that might spring naturally to the lips of any native speaker of English.

Appositive adjectives, which hardly ever spring naturally to our lips, differ from regular adjectives both in placement and in punctuation. They are placed after the noun or before the determiner, and they are set off by commas. When there is no determiner, they are still set off by commas. Their functions are somewhat different, too, although the difference is hard to pin down. It should be fairly easy to feel, however, if you read these three sentences aloud, one after the other.

Adjectives in normal position: The **sturdy old** cabin survived the hurricane.

Appositive adjectives following the noun:	The cabin, **old** but **sturdy,** survived the hurricane.
Appositive adjectives before the determiner:	**Old** but **sturdy,** the cabin survived the hurricane.

In the second and third sentences, the placement and punctuation of *old but sturdy* lead you to place a stress on both appositive adjectives that they do not get in the first sentence. Almost any word out of normal sentence order receives this kind of added stress, which in turn affects its role in a sentence. It is not that the information in *old but sturdy* in the second and third sentences is so different from the information conveyed by *sturdy old* in the first sentence. True, the addition of *but* calls attention to a contrast, but the placement and punctuation of the adjectives focus special attention on the contrast. This is partly because the information is not there primarily to identify the noun. If the adjectives for *cabin* were *old* and *red*—*The old red cabin survived the hurricane*—we would not think of putting *old* and *red* in the appositive position. They describe, they modify, but they do not suggest the same idea as *old but sturdy.* Appositive adjectives typically suggest a relation between information found in a sentence and information carried by the adjectives themselves.

Appositive adjectives hardly ever appear singly (see the examples at the beginning of this chapter). When they do, they are almost always modified by a prepositional phrase, as in the following example, in which the appositive adjective, in boldface, is italicized along with the prepositional phrase modifying it.

> ***Angry*** *over the dirty dishes in the sink,* Jeanette told her roommate she was moving out.

Appositive adjectives do not follow personal pronouns such as *he, she, it,* or *they,* but they may precede them. You may write

> **Witty** and **effervescent,** she was the life of the party.

but if you moved the appositive adjectives after *she,* the sentence would not sound natural.

> ∅She, **witty** and **effervescent,** was the life of the party.

Finally, only appositive adjectives—that is, adjectives set off by commas—may precede proper nouns such as George, Martha, or General Electric. You may write *Honest and kind, Margaret was respected by everybody,* but take away that comma after *kind* and you get a funny-sounding sentence that might be acceptable only in some children's books: *Honest and kind Margaret was respected by everybody.*

How Appositive Adjectives Are Punctuated

As demonstrated in the previous section, punctuation is part of what makes adjectives appositive. They are set off by commas, both when they are placed before a determiner and when they follow the noun they modify.

> **Bubbly** and **newsy,** Janet's letters brightened Juan's days in the war zone.
>
> Janet's letters, **bubbly** and **newsy,** brightened Juan's days in the war zone.

Appositive adjectives may also be set off by dashes.

> Yehuda Amichai's poems—**precise, personal, passionate**—have been translated from Hebrew into thirty-seven languages.

What You Can Do with Appositive Adjectives

1. Control Focus

By being out of normal English word order, appositive adjectives almost automatically receive special focus. This permits you to shine a spotlight on information you want to stress.

> **Intelligent, decisive,** and **fair,** Peggy should make an excellent team leader.
>
> The ocean water, **cool** and **clear,** was irresistible on a hot day.

2. Relate Ideas or Information Economically within a Sentence

As already noted, appositive adjectives typically suggest a relation between information found in a sentence and information carried by the adjectives themselves. They are especially efficient for suggesting cause and effect. In the revision shown here, they replace the original adverb clause in boldface.

> *Original sentence:* Jim's dog is unsafe around little children **because she is overprotective and unpredictable.**
>
> *Revision:* Jim's dog, **overprotective** and **unpredictable,** is unsafe around children.

3. Break up Long Strings of Modifiers

Sometimes two or three modifiers are needed to identify a noun. Adding even more modifiers for description can result in a long string of modifiers. Putting some of them in the appositive position not only breaks up the string but effectively separates modifiers that describe from those that merely identify. In the original sentence of the following example, an italicized string of five modifiers precedes the noun *counselor.* In the revision, the adjectives describing attributes that help explain the counselor's popularity have been separated as appositives from modifiers that merely identify the counselor.

> *Original sentence:* The **energetic, upbeat new assistant camp** counselor was popular with the children.
>
> *Revision:* **Energetic** and **upbeat,** the new assistant camp counselor was popular with the children.

4. Achieve Variety in Sentence Rhythm and Structure

Certain kinds of writing seem to call for many adjectives. When these are in a series of sentences with similar structure, the result can be monotonous; appositive adjectives can break up the structure and rhythm. Compare the paragraphs below reviewing James Baldwin's "Notes of a Native Son."

> *Original:* Baldwin's long, passionate essay is an extraordinary piece of writing. His intricate, sometimes tortured sentences seem to capture raw feelings in conflict with each other. His clear-eyed but compassionate analysis of his father will ring true to many readers whose fathers have been both monstrous and pitiful. His profound, still urgent insights into hatred, which "never failed to destroy the man who hated," should be posted in classrooms around the world.

FIGURE 4.1

Punctuating Appositive Adjectives

Appositive adjectives are set off by punctuation, usually commas.

Energetic and passionate about her subject, the professor kept the class stimulating.
The earthquake, **strong but deep,** did not cause catastrophic damage.

Dashes may also be used (sparingly) to set off appositive adjectives that come after the noun.

Larry's letter of application—**formal but friendly, concise but informative**—won him an interview.

Revision: Baldwin's long, passionate essay is an extraordinary piece of writing. His sentences, **intricate and sometimes tortured,** seem to capture raw feelings in conflict with each other. His clear-eyed but compassionate analysis of his father will ring true to many readers whose fathers have been both monstrous and pitiful. **Profound and still urgent,** his insights into hatred, which "never failed to destroy the man who hated," should be posted in classrooms around the world.

5. Create Coordination and Parallelism

Because they so often come in pairs or in threes, appositive adjectives lend themselves to coordination and parallelism. They can be effectively balanced with correlative coordinate conjunctions such as *neither . . . nor.* On either side of a conjunction such as **but,** and with their own modifiers, they can help compress a complete story into a sentence.

Neither too **formal** nor too **casual,** Selina made a strong impression in her interview.
The minister, **passionate** in the pulpit but **icy** in person, led a lonely existence.
Friendly but **firm, relaxed** but **demanding,** Roy gets a lot of work out of people while keeping morale high.

EXERCISES

A. Practicing Sentence Combining

Combine each group of sentences into one sentence containing appositive adjectives. In each case, the first sentence should remain your base sentence. In some cases you will have to supply coordinating conjunctions (*and, but, or, nor, for, so,* and *yet; either . . . or, neither . . . nor,* and *not [only] . . . but [also]*). In choosing them, think about the meaning of the combined sentence. Experiment with placing the appositive adjectives before and after their nouns. In some cases, you may want to have both appositive and regular adjectives in the same sentence.

Examples

Griselda won the hearts of all who knew her.
Griselda was patient.
Griselda was kind.

Patient and kind, Griselda won the hearts of all who knew her.
or
Griselda, patient and kind, won the hearts of all who knew her.

The retriever won first prize at the Milwaukee Dog Show.
The retriever was a Labrador.
The retriever was young.
The retriever was beautifully groomed.
The retriever was perfectly obedient.
The retriever was from Racine.

Beautifully groomed and perfectly obedient, the young Labrador retriever from Racine won first prize at the Milwaukee Dog Show.
or
The young Labrador retriever from Racine, beautifully groomed and perfectly obedient, won first prize at the Milwaukee Dog Show.

1. The waves battered the beach.
   The waves were huge.
   The waves were savage.

2. A car sat in the driveway.
   It was new.
   It was a sports car.
   It was shiny.

3. The student became instantly unpopular with almost everybody in the class.
   The student was new.
   The student was a music student.
   The student was from Los Angeles.
   The student was loud.
   The student was relentlessly competitive.

4. The secretary of state attracted attention whenever she entered a room.
   She was short.
   She was imposing.

5. Oedipus is sure he will beat the oracle's prediction.
   Oedipus is willful.
   Oedipus is proud.

6. The water was a rich reward for the long hike.
   The water was ocean water.
   The water was green.
   The water was clean.
   The water was inviting.

7. The drama teacher eventually won the devotion of all her students.
   She was strict.
   She was demanding.
   She was kind.

8. The bread went perfectly with the soup.
   The bread was hot.
   The bread was French bread.
   The bread was wonderfully crusty.

9. The tribe was fascinating to study.
   The tribe was economically simple.
   The tribe was socially complex.
   The tribe was an African tribe.
   The tribe was a pygmy tribe.

10. Cliff's brownies were the first item to sell out at the bake sale.
    They were dark.
    They were moist.

11. Richard Wagner's opera *Tristan and Isolde* amply rewards the listener who can get past the intricate, farfetched plot.
    It is long.
    It is demanding.
12. Tristan is bringing Isolde from Ireland to be the bride of his uncle, King Marke of Cornwall.
    Tristan is profoundly loyal.
    Tristan is dutiful.
13. Isolde is the daughter of a line of mighty sorcerers.
    Isolde is proud.
    Isolde is haughty.
14. Isolde prepares a poison mixture with which to kill both Tristan and herself.
    Isolde is furious at Tristan for having captured her for King Marke.
    Isolde is half in love with Tristan from an earlier encounter.
15. Her servant substitutes a love potion for the poison mixture, and Tristan and Isolde drink it.
    Her servant is well-meaning.
    Her servant is shortsighted.
16. Tristan and Isolde rush into one another's arms.
    Tristan and Isolde are helplessly in love.
    Tristan and Isolde are aware that their love is doomed.
17. Tristan and Isolde pour out their love for each other as their ship docks in Cornwall and King Marke prepares to board.
    Tristan and Isolde are oblivious of everything around them.
18. The music of their long love scene rises by slow chromatic steps to an excruciatingly delayed climax.
    The music is almost embarrassing in its sensuality.
19. A series of misunderstandings leads to Tristan's death from wounds inflicted by King Marke's lieutenant, Melot.
    The misunderstandings are avoidable.
    The misunderstandings are thus all the more tragic.
20. The love-scene music returns in the famous Liebestod ("love-death"), which Isolde sings over Tristan's body before she falls upon him.
    Isolde is dead of a broken heart.

B. Writing Your Own Appositive Adjectives

1. Write five sentences that use appositive adjectives following the noun they modify. (Example: *The children, happy but hungry after the long hike, ate ravenously.*)
2. Write five sentences that use appositive adjectives before the noun they modify. (Example: *Polite but distant, Gerhard made it clear that he still bore a grudge.*)

C. Appositive Adjectives in Published Writing

Here is a passage by writer Ralph Ellison about the great blues singer Jimmy Rushing. Locate the appositive adjectives in the passage and comment on their use. How might the same information be conveyed without appositive adjectives? Compare the effects of other possible phrasings with the effect of the original.

> In the old days, the voice was high and clear and poignantly lyrical. Steel-bright in its upper range, and, at its best, silky smooth, it was possessed of a purity somehow impervious to both the stress of singing above a twelve-piece band and the urgency of Rushing's own blazing fervor. On dance nights, when you stood on the rise of the school grounds two blocks to the east, you could hear it jetting from the dance hall like a blue flame in the dark.
>
> Ralph Ellison, "Remembering Jimmy" in *Shadow and Act* (New York: Signet Books, 1966), 235.

D. Combining in Context

Revise the following paragraphs with special attention to the adjectives in noun phrases. Would it be an improvement to move some adjectives into the appositive position? Are there some opportunities to emphasize differences, similarities, or other connections by joining adjectives with coordinate or correlative conjunctions or by placing them in parallel structures?

1. Cyril could not believe it was happening. All those empty seats in the Greyhound bus and this striking young woman chose the seat next to his. Every feature was perfect. Her abundant, jet-black hair came

almost to her shoulders and then curled elegantly upward. Her dark, mysterious eyes were at the same time friendly. Her high, prominent cheekbones gave her face a regal look. Her delicate, shapely nose reminded him of the Song of Solomon. Her full, sensual, naturally red lips curved slightly upward in a permanent modest half-smile that widened into a dazzling full smile as she asked, "Excuse me. May I sit here, or is this seat taken?" "No, I mean yes, I mean no," said Cyril, hating himself. His response brought a delighted musical laugh out of her throat. "I do that all the time, too," she said. This beautiful and also kind woman seemed to be everything Cyril had always dreamed of. He was in love.

2. The teenagers at the Manzanar internment camp in 1942 were Japanese in origin but American in everything else. They played touch football, tried out for cheerleading squads, and performed Glen Miller arrangements in their bands. They also took advantage of camp life to taste the freedom of American children. Mealtimes could no longer be traditional affairs around a table presided over by a patriarchal father. Camp residents ate at long tables in mess halls, and family members would scatter in search of mess halls with shorter lines or better food. The more ambitious ones would get second meals by moving between early servings at one mess hall and later ones at another. For the children, this was fun. For their fathers, it was another blow to their manly pride. Their fathers were already angry and depressed. According to Jeanne Wakatsuki Houston in *Farewell to Manzanar,* the final "snip of the castrator's scissors" came upon their return home from the camps. Her father found his car repossessed and his fishing boats gone without any records. He was impoverished. He was emasculated. He never recovered his faith in himself or in the country to which he had come so full of energy and hope.

E. Revising Your Writing for Style

Choose a piece of your own writing and examine it for its use of adjectives, looking especially for places where appositive adjectives might be effective. (Because appositive adjectives rarely appear singly, you may need to add a second adjective or add a prepositional phrase to modify a single adjective.) Locate adjectives in noun phrases and ask yourself the following questions.

1. Are there places where you could put more of a spotlight on some quality you want the reader to pay attention to? Could you do this by putting adjectives in the appositive position?
2. Are there places where you could use appositive adjectives to suggest relations between ideas or information? For instance, is there a clause beginning with *because* that could be reduced to appositive adjectives?
3. Are there any long strings of modifiers that could be broken up?
4. Are there places where appositive adjectives could help bring about more variety in sentence structure and rhythm?
5. Are there places where coordinate or parallel structures could help reflect coordinate or parallel ideas?

Chapter 5

Compound Sentences

What Compound Sentences Look Like

1. The trapeze artists went into their final leap, and the crowd held its breath.
2. The team wanted to keep Matthews, but his salary demands had zoomed too high.
3. DNA studies have found that Thomas Jefferson fathered at least one son by his slave Sally Hemmings, and the Thomas Jefferson Memorial Foundation has accepted the finding, but some of his white descendants remain sturdily unconvinced.
4. The temperature was 14°F, the Super Bowl was in full swing, and the streets of the city were empty.
5. Sheila could not reach Christina all day, so Sheila drove to the party alone.
6. Few people prefer reading onscreen to reading on paper, for onscreen text clarity remains very inferior.

7. Either you will start doing your share of the housework, or you will find another place to live.
8. The city made an extraordinary effort to clear away the snow and ice; ten thousand tons of salt were poured on the streets in one day.
9. Igor eats to live; Yuri lives to eat.
10. The *eToys.com* site says you must be eighteen to create a gift registry; however, all you need is an email address.
11. On April 9, 1940, Norwegians woke up to shocking news: Germany had invaded their country.
12. After ten years of public service, he was a very wealthy man—and people were asking questions.

How Grammarians Describe Compound Sentences

Any sentence element—subject, verb, direct object, modifier, and even the independent clause—can be compounded. That is, it can appear in a pair or in a series. Such elements are said to be coordinate—that is, grammatically equal. When a sentence contains more than one independent clause and no dependent clause, it is called a **compound sentence.** Each sentence in the next list contains compound elements, but only the last sentence is a compound sentence because the elements in boldface are independent clauses—that is, they could stand alone as sentences.

Compound subject:	**People** and **bears** coexist warily in the Yukon.
Compound verb:	Jack **fell** down and **broke** his crown.
Compound direct object:	Pinchas Zuckermann plays the **violin** and the **viola** with equal skill.
Compound modifier:	The **green** and **fertile** valley was home to many farmers.
Compound sentence:	**Thunder rattled the windows,** and **the dog dove under the bed.**

Coordinate independent clauses may be joined by **coordinating conjunctions, coordinating correlative conjunctions,** or certain punctuation marks

FIGURE 5.1

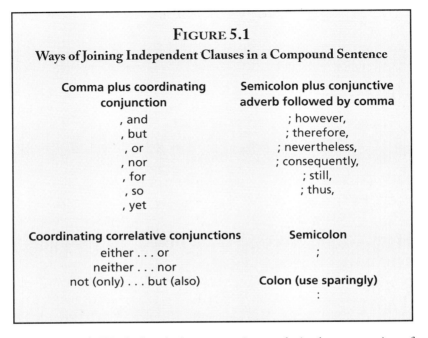

Ways of Joining Independent Clauses in a Compound Sentence

Comma plus coordinating conjunction	**Semicolon plus conjunctive adverb followed by comma**
, and	; however,
, but	; therefore,
, or	; nevertheless,
, nor	; consequently,
, for	; still,
, so	; thus,
, yet	

Coordinating correlative conjunctions	**Semicolon**
either . . . or	;
neither . . . nor	
not (only) . . . but (also)	**Colon (use sparingly)**
	:

(see figure 5.1). We deal with the punctuation marks in the next section of this chapter. The list of coordinating conjunctions is short: *and, but, or, nor, for, so,* and *yet.* Some people remember the list by rearranging the coordinating conjunctions so that their first letters spell "fanboys" (whatever those are!). Note that the list does not include *however, therefore,* and *nevertheless,* which are called **conjunctive adverbs** and which cannot be used by themselves to coordinate clauses. They can be used with semicolons (see sentence 10 at the beginning of this chapter) and also with coordinating conjunctions, as in, *and therefore* and *but nevertheless. So* and *yet,* in the words of grammarian Martha Kolln, "straddle the border between the coordinating conjunctions and the conjunctive adverbs";[1] they can be used either alone or with *and* or *but,* as in *and so* and *but yet.*

Coordinating correlative conjunctions come in pairs: *either. . . or, neither. . . nor,* and *not (only). . . but (also).* These are used most often with elements shorter than independent clauses, such as compound subjects (*Neither*

[1]Martha Kolln, *Understanding English Grammar,* 3d ed. (New York: Macmillan, 1990), 249.

*the **Rams** nor the **Titans** put on a stellar performance.*), but they can also be used to join independent clauses.

> Either **Jane and Richard will fly together,** or **Richard will come two days later.**

Compound sentences may be **elliptical;** that is, certain grammatically necessary words may be omitted and interpreted as understood. The omitted words may include the coordinating conjunction and other sentence elements such as the verb or even the subject.

> The sand was pearl white, [and] the sea [was] emerald green.
> In one hand, he held the baby's bottle, [and] in the other, [he held] the cell phone.
> The Clagetts were diehard liberals and their children [were] diehard conservatives.

How Compound Sentences Are Punctuated

The most common way to join two independent clauses is to use a coordinating conjunction preceded by a comma.

> The regular teacher was out sick, **and** the class was tormenting the substitute.

With compound elements that are not independent clauses, we do not use a comma before the conjunction. Here, for instance, is a compound predicate.

> The guests **did not notice the time** ***and*** **stayed until two in the morning.**

The comma before the conjunction joining independent clauses is important: It signals to readers that a new independent clause is coming after the conjunction and thus helps them read accurately. An educated reader's brain is programmed to expect different continuations from the following two beginnings.

> The earth exerts gravitational force on the moon **and** . . .
> The earth exerts gravitational force on the moon, **and** . . .

The comma with the conjunction between independent clauses becomes especially important when there are other conjunctions nearby.

> Drivers abandoned their cars in the face of snow *and* sleet, **and** buses *and* trains were full to capacity.

The comma before the conjunction in a compound sentence does indicate a little break between one clause and the next. When you want no break at all—for instance, to indicate that one thing followed hard upon another—and when the clauses are short, you can get away with omitting the comma before the coordinating conjunction.

> The Rams won the Super Bowl **and** I lost twenty dollars.

The comma is also sometimes omitted from elliptical compound sentences when the conjunction is used.

> The climbers' physical condition was perfect **and** their training superb.

But these are exceptions to the rule that should govern your normal practice: use a comma before the coordinating conjunction joining independent clauses in a compound sentence.

The independent clauses of a compound sentence may also be joined by semicolons. Semicolons are most useful for pointing up a close relation between ideas or between equal parts of a single idea. When you use semicolons, you do not need a coordinating conjunction.

> Sims was reappointed with no opposition; everybody is happy with the job he is doing.
>
> Patriotism is not a refusal to find fault with your country; it is the belief that your country can live up to its ideals.

There is no rule against using a coordinating conjunction when you also use a semicolon. This can be useful when there are commas inside the clauses being joined.

> People predicted that the new law would create confusion, curtail essential public services, and have other unintended consequences; **and** within a short time, they were proved right.

Two less conventional but useful punctuation marks for joining independent clauses are the colon and the dash. A colon is a slightly more formal way of signaling that an example or explanation is to follow.

> After years of spectacular rises in the prices of stocks, the inevitable happened: their prices plummeted.

A dash is a slightly more informal punctuation mark. It signals a bigger break than is indicated by a comma and can place added significance on the clause that follows it.

> Oprah's Book Club choices are weighted in favor of novels involving women in personal crises—and this has not been lost on publishers.

Both the colon and the dash are best used sparingly, but they should not be avoided. Punctuation can do a lot to help readers read your sentences as you want the sentences to be read.

In the following sentence, the writer effectively uses both a colon and semicolon to reflect the structure of his idea.

> "I understand the frustration the feminist pioneers must have felt: clam up and nothing changes; speak up and they label you noisy and nuts." (Bruce Kluger, "Breaking through the Estrogen Ceiling," *Newsweek,* Jan. 31, 2000, 11.)

Sometimes you will find *and* or *but* placed not between the clauses of a compound sentence but at the beginning of a separate sentence.

> She was beautiful, popular, and wealthy. **And** she cried herself to sleep every night.

There is no rule against beginning a sentence with *and* or *but;* professional writers have been doing it since the beginning of written English. However, this is done for a special stylistic or rhetorical effect: it puts a spotlight on a sentence and on its relation to the one preceding it. As with all special effects, the way to keep it special is to use it sparingly and with good reason.

What You Can Do with Compound Sentences

1. Connect Two or More Events or Ideas

This is a basic function of the compound sentence with *and.* If overused, it can make writing sound childish. Used sparingly, however, it is a simple, efficient way of letting readers view things together and draw their own conclusions about the relation among the parts, which are often obvious.

> It was spring, **and** the park was full of young lovers.
>
> School boards demand test results of principals, **and** principals demand them of teachers.
>
> He is an accountant, she is an economist, **and** neither can balance a checkbook.

2. Vary Sentence Length within a Paragraph

Successful writers use sentences of different lengths for variety and effect. Compound sentences are a useful tool for this purpose. When you want to break up a series of short sentences, it is sometimes enough simply to join some of them into compound sentences.

> *Original:* The soldiers' motivation was high. Their discipline was superb. They were ready to show their mettle. Soon they would have a chance.
>
> *Revision:* The soldiers' motivation was high, their discipline superb. They were ready to show their mettle, and soon they would have a chance.

3. Help Your Reader Navigate a Long Sentence

Sometimes, a single subject may have two extended predicates, which can be confusing to readers because they may not remember the subject by the time they get to the second predicate.

> *Today's immigrants* come to an America different in many ways from that of the late nineteenth and early twentieth centuries **and** face a different set of challenges.

Turning this into a compound sentence gives readers a break after the first predicate and then supplies a fresh subject—the pronoun *they*—to be the subject of the second predicate.

> *Today's immigrants* come to an America different in many ways from that of the late nineteenth and early twentieth centuries**, and** *they* face a different set of challenges.

4. Create Coordination and Parallelism

Compound sentences are coordinate by definition. Making whole independent clauses parallel can put similarities, contrasts, and other relations into stark relief.

> **I moved to New York out of necessity,** but **I remained there out of love.**
>
> In some regions, **people of low income could not afford to live in the suburbs;** today **they cannot afford to live in the cities.**

FIGURE 5.2
Punctuating Compound Sentences

Comma plus coordinate conjunction (*and, but, or, nor, for, yet, so*)

Comma plus coordinating correlative conjunctions (*either . . . or, not [only] . . . but [also]*)

Semicolon plus conjunctive adverb followed by comma (. . . ; *however,* . . .)

Semicolon

Colon or dash (use sparingly)

"**Dryden often surpasses expectation,** and **Pope never falls below it. Dryden is read with frequent astonishment,** and **Pope with perpetual delight.**" [Samuel Johnson, *Lives of the Poets* (1781). Reprinted in *The Norton Anthology of English Literature,* ed. M. H. Abrams (New York: W. W. Norton, 1979), 1: 2376.]

EXERCISES

A. Practicing Sentence Combining

Combine each group of sentences into one compound sentence. There may be other ways to combine the groups, but here practice writing compound sentences. Experiment with different ways of combining the groups.

Examples

The kick would have meant victory for Garfield High.
Julian miraculously blocked it.

The kick would have meant victory for Garfield High, and Julian miraculously blocked it.

or

The kick would have meant victory for Garfield High, but Julian miraculously blocked it.

My old hair stylist started charging $65 for a simple cut.
I found another stylist.

My hair stylist started charging $65 for a simple cut, so I found another stylist.

or

I found another hair stylist, for my old one started charging $65 for a simple cut.

Tracy needed total darkness to fall asleep.
Marlowe needed to read to fall asleep.
Neither seemed able to compromise.

Tracy needed total darkness to fall asleep, Marlowe needed to read to fall asleep, and neither seemed able to compromise.

or

Tracy needed total darkness to fall asleep, and Marlowe needed to read to fall asleep, and neither seemed able to compromise.

or

Tracy needed total darkness to fall asleep, and Marlowe needed to read to fall asleep; neither seemed able to compromise.

1. It was the day before Valentine's Day.
   The lines outside Fran's Chocolates stretched around the block.
2. The Mayor tried to have both freedom and order on the streets.
   He ended up having repression and chaos.
3. Orlando was a superb cook.
   Julio was a superb gardener.
   Neither of them could bear to clean house.
4. The family was, as usual, evenly divided over vacation plans.
   Dad wanted to go to Maine.
   Mom wanted to go to the Jersey Shore.
   Jesse wanted to go nowhere.
5. Solomon had no way of knowing who the real mother was.
   He found a way of making her reveal herself.
6. Some people assumed F. Scott Fitzgerald was shallow and stupid.
   They could not separate the author from his characters.
7. She is a skilled administrator and a prizewinning poet.
   This is not all.
   She is also an accomplished mountain climber and an expert mechanic.

8. On his first date, Rudy left nothing to chance.
   He even rented a car because his was unreliable.
9. According to Dostoevsky's Grand Inquisitor, people do not desire freedom.
   People desire bread, mystery, and authority.
10. Felix's mother was also his math teacher.
    However, she cut him no slack when marking his tests.

In combining the next set of sentence groups, you may want to try substituting a pronoun for the subject in the second clause, but only if the reference is totally unambiguous.

11. The class trip was supposed to include a visit to a volcano.
    The visit was canceled.
12. Seismologists had recorded underground rumblings.
    The seismologists advised against approaching the volcano.
13. Were the rumblings the voices of the gods, as some people believed?
    Were the rumblings merely the result of the underground movement of molten rock?
14. At its last eruption, the volcano created a river of melted snow.
    The river swept seven people to their deaths.
15. The last eruption was in 1985, when I was ten years old.
    The eruption is only a vague memory for me.
16. Authorities warned people to clear the area.
    Many people were not very smart.
17. Good luck can save people from their own stupidity for a long time.
    In an emergency, their own stupidity will often catch up with them.
18. Gamblers think we live in a world where luck rules.
    Dreamers think we live in a world where wishing makes it so.
    Both gamblers and dreamers are wrong.
19. Actions have consequences.
    Consequences must be considered before we take actions.
20. People who disregarded this truth ignored a clear warning.
    The truth was brought home to them in a violent way.

B. Writing Your Own Compound Sentences

1. Write three compound sentences, each with a different coordinating conjunction. Do not forget to place a comma before the coordinating conjunction. (Example: *Airline fares are getting higher, but airline seats are getting smaller.*)
2. Write three compound sentences, each using a semicolon plus a conjunctive adverb followed by a comma. Use a different conjunctive adverb for each one. (Example: *Newtonian dynamics has been replaced by Einstein's relativity theory; however, Newton's laws still work well enough to guide spacecraft to the moon.*)
3. Write three compound sentences each using a semicolon to join the clauses. (Example: *Felix does not believe in hiring family members for his firm; in his experience, it always leads to problems.*)

C. Compound Sentences in Published Writing

Here is a passage by writer David Brooks. Locate the compound sentences in the passage and comment on their use. How might the same information be conveyed without compound sentences? Compare the effects of other possible phrasings with the effect of the original.

> In our conversations I would ask the [Princeton] students when they got around to sleeping. One senior told me that she went to bed around two and woke up each morning at seven; she could afford that much rest because she had learned to supplement her full day of work by studying in her sleep. As she was falling asleep she would recite a math problem or a paper topic to herself; she would then sometimes dream about it, and when she woke up, the problem might be solved. I asked several students to describe their daily schedules, and their replies sounded like a session of future Workaholics of America: crew practice at dawn, classes in the morning, resident-adviser duty, lunch, study groups, classes in the afternoon, tutoring disadvantaged kids in Trenton, a cappella practice, dinner, study, science lab, prayer session, hit the StairMaster, study a few hours more. One young man told me that he had to schedule appointment times for chatting with his friends. I mentioned this to other groups, and usually one or two people would volunteer that they did the same thing. "I just had an appointment with my best

friend at seven this morning," one woman said. "Or else you lose touch."

There are a lot of things these future leaders no longer have time for. I was on campus at the height of the election season, and I saw not even one Bush or Gore poster. I asked around about this and was told that most students have no time to read newspapers, follow national politics, or get involved in crusades. One senior told me that she had subscribed to *The New York Times* once, but the papers had just piled up unread in her dorm room. . . . Even the biological necessities get squeezed out. I was amazed to learn how little dating goes on. Students go out in groups, and there is certainly a fair bit of partying on campus, but as one told me, "People don't have time or energy to put into real relationships."

David Brooks, "The Organization Kid,"
The Atlantic Monthly, April (2001), 40.

D. Combining in Context

Rewrite the following paragraphs, making effective use of compound sentences to indicate relations, emphasize similarities and differences, vary sentence length, and improve clarity.

1. Bernal Diaz, author of *The Conquest of New Spain,* entered Tenochtitlan—today's Mexico City—with Hernando Cortéz in November 1519. Diaz could hardly believe his eyes. Before him there stretched a teeming metropolis of 500,000. No European city even approached that number. Tenochtitlan had been built over a salt marsh. It was crisscrossed by canals. The solidly built bridges over the canals were broader than any bridges Diaz had seen. Ten horsemen could easily ride abreast over them. A large, sophisticatedly engineered aqueduct carried pure water from distant springs and supplied fountains in the parks. Every kind of merchandise was on display in the marketplaces. Some of it, especially the gold and silver work, was of remarkable splendor. Food was varied and abundant. You could buy turkeys, rabbits, deer, beans, corn, peppers, and much more. On one side of the central square of Tenochtitlan stood the great temple of Huitzilopochtli. It was 100 feet high from its enormous base and approached by three flights of 120 steps each. In November 1519, Cortéz himself stood in awe of the Aztec empire. Within two years he had destroyed it.

2. Alternative medicine has become big business in the United States. It is finally getting serious attention from medical researchers. Treatments from acupuncture to shark cartilage are being measured by the same method used for standard Western treatments. They are being tested in large studies using control groups and placebos. This is not always simple. How do you pretend to give someone acupuncture? In one University of Maryland study, a control group received needle sticks in places where, according to traditional Chinese medicine, they should not do any good. At the University of Michigan, researchers are studying the Chinese art of qi gong, a slow-motion exercise that is said to release a healing energy. The University of Michigan study tests the benefits of qi gong for patients recovering from cardiac surgery. One-third of the patients will be visited by a qi gong master. One-third will be visited by an imposter. One-third will receive no visits at all. For some scientists, this research is long overdue. They believe it could add effective new therapies to current medical practice. For others, it is a waste of money. One scientist calls such therapies "quackupuncture." Perhaps the research will demonstrate only that faith heals. Perhaps this is the most useful knowledge of all.

E. Revising Your Writing for Style

Choose a piece of your own writing and revise it using compound sentences where these would be effective. Consider these questions when you think about revising.

1. Are there places where you can use coordinating conjunctions or punctuation marks to point out relations among events or ideas?
2. Are there places where similarities or contrasts could be emphasized by compound sentences?
3. Are there places where you can vary sentence length within a paragraph by using compound sentences?
4. Are there places where compounding might help your reader navigate a long sentence?
5. Are there places where parallel structure could help reflect parallel ideas?

CHAPTER 6

RELATIVE CLAUSES

WHAT RELATIVE CLAUSES LOOK LIKE

1. Joseph led the band of Nez Perce **that lived in the Wallowas.**
2. General Howard finally defeated the Nez Perce, **whom he admired greatly.**
3. The Wallowas, **in which the Nez Perce spent their summers,** are snow-capped peaks until midsummer.
4. The Wallowas, **which the Nez Perce spent their summers in,** are snow-capped peaks until midsummer.
5. Joseph prepared the women and children **he led** for flight.
6. Ollokot, **whose fighting skills were well known,** was the warrior leader of Joseph's band.
7. The treaty **whose terms Joseph's band was refusing to sign** took away land given them by the first treaty between the United States and the Nez Perce.

8. In 1806, **when Lewis and Clark spent a month with the Nez Perce,** Old Joseph, the father of the man we now know as Chief Joseph, was a boy.
9. In Lapwai, **where Spalding built a mission for the Nez Perce,** there is now a National Park Service Museum.
10. We can give several reasons **why the Nez Perce and the negotiators for the United States did not understand one another.**
11. Many Native American leaders were called "chief" by the Americans, **which showed a misunderstanding of Native American culture.**

HOW GRAMMARIANS DESCRIBE RELATIVE CLAUSES

Relative clauses, which are a type of dependent clause (see chapter 1), are also known as adjective or adjectival clauses because they function as adjectives in a sentence. They are introduced by a group of words called **relative pronouns** (figure 6.1). Like **personal pronouns,** these relative pronouns refer to a noun; they usually come immediately after the noun that they refer to; unlike personal pronouns, relative pronouns function as the beginning of a dependent clause. In addition to introducing a relative clause, the relative pronoun functions in its own clause as a subject, direct object, object of a preposition, or possessive. This accounts for the different forms *who, whom,* and *whose* (see the pronoun chart in appendix D). There are also a few adverbs that sometimes function to introduce relative clauses and are then called **relative adverbs,** as in sentences 8, 9, and 10 at the beginning of the chapter. Usually, *who* and *whom* refer to people, *which* refers to things, and *that* can refer to either. When the relative pronoun functions as the object in its clause, it may be omitted as in sentence 5.

In one variation of the relative clause, the relative pronoun refers not to just one word but to the idea of an entire independent clause. In this use of *which* to introduce a relative clause, there seems to be an implied phrase, *a fact,* which the relative pronoun refers to.

> The president was less than truthful with the American people, [a fact] **which was clear to everyone.**

In written English, some people frown on this use of the relative clause; certainly we should be careful that the broad-reference *which* does not seem to

FIGURE 6.1

Words That Begin Relative Clauses

Relative pronouns	**Relative adverbs**
who, whose, whom	when
which	where
that	why

refer to the word that comes immediately before it and that *a fact* could be inserted. Clearly in the next sentence, the relative clause does not work.

> ∅I walked to town yesterday, **which was the first time this year.**

HOW RELATIVE CLAUSES ARE PUNCTUATED

The hardest part of relative clauses is their punctuation, which is based on the distinction between **restrictive** and **nonrestrictive** modifiers (see figure 6.2). However, with some definitions and a little thought, you will find that the punctuation is not all that difficult.

When we speak we use timing and pitch almost automatically to distinguish between restrictive and nonrestrictive clauses, but when we write we must use punctuation to make the distinction. The rule is that restrictive clauses are not set off with commas, and nonrestrictive clauses are. The rule is easy enough to say, but what does it mean? Let us look at some examples.

> Interstate 5, **which cuts Seattle in half,** was built in 1962.
> The street **that** [or **which**] **runs in front of my house** needs repaving once a month.

In the first sentence, we do not need the information in the relative clause to tell us which Interstate 5 cuts Seattle in half because there is only one Interstate 5 in Seattle, so the clause is nonrestrictive; it comments on the word that it modifies. In the second sentence, we do need the information about the street running in front of my house to tell us which street we mean because innumerable streets might need repaving once a month, so the

FIGURE 6.2
Restrictive and Nonrestrictive Modifiers

Restrictive: The information in the relative clause is necessary to distinguish the noun that it modifies from all similar things to which the noun might be referring.

> The Native American tribes **that live in Washington state** won a major victory in the Boldt Decision.

Nonrestrictive: The information in the relative clause is not necessary to distinguish the noun because this is already clear.

> The city of Spokane, **which is located on the Spokane River in eastern Washington state,** is named after a Native American tribe.

clause is restrictive; it distinguishes the word that it modifies from similar things it might be referring to, in this case the other streets that do not run in front of my house.

Here is another pair.

> People **who live in Los Angeles** must breathe polluted air.
> People, **who must breathe air,** have no choice but to breathe polluted air when they live in Los Angeles.

In the first sentence, we need the information about exactly which people we are talking about; not all people must breathe polluted air. Thus, the relative clause in the first sentence is restrictive. In the second sentence, the information that people must breathe air is not necessary to tell us which people we are talking about; all people must breathe air. The information is in the sentence for emphasis. The relative clause in the second sentence is nonrestrictive. It might be helpful to think about how you would say the two sentences and note the differences between restrictive and nonrestrictive in spoken English.

Here is one last pair.

> My sister **who lives in San Francisco** is a nurse.
> My sister, **who lives in San Francisco,** is a nurse.

In the first sentence, I have more than one sister, so the information is necessary to indicate which sister I mean; the relative clause is restrictive. In the second sentence, I have only one sister, so the information about where she lives is extra, unnecessary for determining which sister I mean; the clause is nonrestrictive.

Notice that proper nouns are almost always modified by nonrestrictive clauses because the proper noun names a specific person, place, or thing; therefore we know which person, place, or thing we are referring to. The only exception to this occurs when there are two persons, places, or things with the same name and there is a possible confusion about which one we are referring to. In this case, the noun is preceded by *the.*

> *The* Julie **who** (or **that**) **sits in the front row** is my sister.
> *The* Columbus **that** (or **which**) **is in Ohio** is the home of Ohio State University.

Another piece of information is important here. When introducing a relative clause, *that* is used to introduce restrictive clauses only. In other words, relative clauses beginning with *that* will never be set off with commas. As difficult as the punctuation rules for restrictive and nonrestrictive clauses may seem because of the difficulty of determining whether the clause is restrictive or nonrestrictive, most native speakers of English use *that* correctly to begin only restrictive clauses, and that has been going on since Anglo-Saxon times.

Some editors and English teachers consider the use of *which* to begin restrictive clauses an error. This is one of the grammar conventions we mentioned in chapter 1. The historical record of the written language is full of examples of *which* used with restrictive clauses, but the prejudice against it remains strong.

Finally, relative clauses that modify the whole sentence are always set off with a comma, perhaps because they are in some way nonrestrictive or perhaps because of the timing and pitch change when the clauses are spoken. The punctuation here is a reminder that punctuation follows syntax, but it is also a matter of convention for the written language.

You should also note that the same restrictive/nonrestrictive rule applies to appositive nouns (chapter 3) and to participle phrases (chapter 10) that come after the nouns they modify.

What You Can Do with Relative Clauses

1. Maintain Paragraph Flow and Focus

Relative clauses are particularly useful for adding to a sentence pertinent, helpful, and even necessary information that would interrupt the flow and focus of a paragraph and/or cause unhelpful repetition if it were in a separate sentence.

> Leon climbed Mt. Si when he was five. Mt. Si is near Seattle, Washington. On his twelfth birthday he climbed Mt. Rainier.
>
> Leon climbed Mt. Si, **which is near Seattle, Washington,** when he was five. On his twelfth birthday he climbed Mt. Rainier.

When we use relative clauses for this kind of information, it is important to keep the information that is the main focus of the sentence, and therefore of the paragraph, in the independent clause; the information needing less emphasis goes in the dependent relative clause. In the next sentences, the focus changes when the information changes from dependent to independent clause.

> Arnold Schwarzenegger, **who always dreamed of being a rich American and living in California,** was born in a small town in Austria.
>
> Arnold Schwarzenegger, **who was born in a small town in Austria,** always dreamed of being a rich American and living in California.

The first sentence emphasizes where Schwarzenegger was born. We expect it to be followed by further information about the town and Schwarzenegger's life there. The second sentence emphasizes Schwarzenegger's dream, and we expect it to be followed by further information about the dream.

Here is another example of keeping the focus with a relative clause.

> The tragedy **that brought her life to an end** was only the final tragedy in a life of tragedies.

Usually this is more effective than using two separate sentences.

> A tragedy brought her life to an end. It was the final tragedy in a life of tragedies.

2. Create Coordination and Parallelism

Relative clauses may be used in a series to add information that needs more than one verb phrase or even to add emphasis when the same verb phrase is used.

FIGURE 6.3
Punctuating Relative Clauses

Restrictive relative clauses are not punctuated.

Snow White bit into the apple **that the wicked queen gave her.**

Nonrestrictive relative clauses are set off by commas.

Granny Smith apples, **which are grown all over the world,** were originally cultivated in New Zealand.

A man **who is kind, who is honest,** and **who makes a good living** is already taken.

Relative clauses may also be used to make balanced sentences; when the meaning implies a balance, the sentence structure can reinforce that balance.

Sometimes the person **that we date** is not the same person **that we marry.**

EXERCISES

A. Practicing Sentence Combining

Combine each group of sentences into one sentence that uses at least one relative clause. The starred sentence should be emphasized (be the independent clause).

Example

*The apricots must be ripe.
You use the apricots for apricot jam.

The apricots that you use for apricot jam must be ripe.

1. *Children play in the street.
The children have nowhere else to play.
The street is busy.

2. *I was glad to meet the woman.
   The woman's cake won first prize at the fair.
3. *The people have a rock band.
   The people live next door.
4. *Interstate 5 was damaged in the last Los Angeles earthquake.
   Interstate 5 runs north and south between Canada and Mexico.
5. *Puerto Vallarta is on the Pacific Coast of Mexico.
   I am going to Puerto Vallarta for my vacation.
6. Rio de Janeiro is known for its *Carnaval.*
   *Rio de Janeiro is the second largest city of Brazil.
7. *The Middle Ages was a time.
   In that time, English underwent great changes.
8. **L'Avventura* both bored and captivated audiences.
   L'Avventura's director, Antonioni, died in 1994.
9. *Sam Shepard has called country music the only really adult music.
   Country music's theme is lost loves.
   Country music's theme is lost lives.
10. *The raven is a large completely black bird.
    The raven is important in folktales and mythologies around the world.
11. *Fish wheels depleted the salmon runs by about 5 percent at the end of the nineteenth century.
    Fish wheels caught the salmon in buckets and dumped them out of the river.
12. Salmon canneries were very profitable for a short period of time.
    *Salmon canneries hired large numbers of Chinese workers.
13. *The Chinese workers could can a ton of salmon per hour.
    Each worker could clean a salmon in forty-five seconds.
14. *A machine replaced the Chinese workers.
    The machine worked much faster than any human could.
15. *The machine was itself soon to be useless.
    The machine replaced Chinese workers.
16. *Fish wheels were finally banned in Oregon and Washington.
    Fish wheels are merely symptomatic of our overuse of natural resources.

17. The salmon runs had been depleted by 50 percent before the dams were built.
    *The salmon runs are now at crisis levels.
18. *The salmon enter the Columbia from the Pacific Ocean.
    The salmon have 25 percent body fat to begin their trip upstream.
19. *Spawning streams are too warm for the salmon's cold-blooded system.
    The temperature in the spawning streams now reaches 70°F in September.
20. *The salmon return to their home stream.
    The home stream is where they lay their eggs.
    The home stream is where they die.

B. Writing Your Own Relative Clauses

1. Write five sentences that correctly use *who* to begin a relative clause. (Example: *Jeremy, who has not danced in years, left his wife for a dancer.*)
2. Write five sentences that correctly use *whom* to begin a relative clause. (Example: *The suspect whom the police have been seeking for three years was finally caught.*)
3. Write five sentences that correctly use *that* to begin a relative clause. (Example: *The windows that I washed yesterday will be dirty again soon.*)
4. Write five sentences that use relative adverbs to begin a relative clause. (Example: *There was a time when Pennsylvania was heavily forested.*)

C. Relative Clauses in Published Writing

Here is a passage by writer Ian Frazier. Locate the relative clauses in the passage and comment on their use. How might the same information be conveyed without relative clauses? Compare the effects of other possible phrasings with the effect of the original.

> On another corner is the Pine Ridge post office, which shares a large brick building with an auditorium called Billy Mills Hall, where most of the important indoor community gatherings are held. On another corner is a two-story brick building containing tribal offices and the offices of the Oglala Department of Public Safety—the

tribal police. . . . On another corner is a combination convenience store and gas station that then was called Big Bat's Conoco and now is called Big Bat's Texaco. Le and I parked and went in.

Ian Frazier, "On the Rez," *The Atlantic Monthly,* December 1999, 68.

D. Combining in Context

In the following paragraphs, change one or more of the independent clauses to relative clauses in order to improve paragraph coherence.

1. The Pueblo united briefly to drive the Spanish from their lands. The Pueblo had no history of confederacy for any reason. When their religion was suppressed beyond their endurance, they finally began to listen to ideas of confederacy. A San Juan Pueblo medicine man named Popé was flogged and driven from San Juan Pueblo. The Spanish were numerous in the San Juan Pueblo area. He went to the more distant pueblo of Taos and from there helped direct the revolt. He communicated with the other pueblos including the Hopi by sending around a piece of cloth with knots. The knots indicated the exact day of the revolt. On that day, each pueblo rose, attacked, and killed the friar assigned to it and whatever Spanish soldiers and colonists they could. Then they moved toward Santa Fe with their Apache allies to drive out the Spanish. About 1,700 Spanish soldiers and colonists were driven out of Pueblo country and across the Rio Grande at what is today El Paso/Juarez. It was sixteen years before the Spanish recovered their position in the Pueblo area; they never reestablished control over the Hopi.
2. In 1869 John Wesley Powell led an expedition of nine men and four boats down the Colorado River and through the Grand Canyon. John Wesley Powell lost his right arm in the Civil War. For seventeen days they ran the river, gliding past hills and ledges, sweeping past sharp angles. The angles jutted out into the river. When they stopped briefly on a patch of dry or wet sand at the river's edge, they ate from their remaining food supply—unleavened biscuits, spoiled bacon, and lots of coffee. Then they returned to the river. The river roared constantly in their ears. Sometimes they had difficult portages; these portages kept them to five miles a day. Sometimes portage was impossible, so

they stayed in the river, shooting the rapids, swirling in eddies, making thirty-five miles a day. In his journal, Powell describes the Grand Canyon as a granite prison. In some places it rose a mile above the river. Three of the men could endure it no more and left the expedition on August 28 for an overland trip. On August 30, 1869, the remaining six men emerged from the canyon into open sky. That evening they sat around the campfire, talking of the Grand Canyon, talking of home, but talking chiefly of the three men. The men had left them. They learned later that the three men managed to climb out of the canyon but were killed by Native Americans. The Native Americans mistook them for miners. The miners had killed a Native American woman. A couple of years after this trip, Powell made another trip down the Grand Canyon and then turned his journals of the two trips into a book, *Explorations of the Colorado River.* The book was published in 1875.

E. Revising Your Writing for Style

Choose a piece of your own writing and revise it using relative clauses where these would be effective. Consider the following questions when you think about revising.

1. Is there information interrupting the flow of your paragraphs that would fit in a relative clause?
2. Are there places where you could use a series of relative clauses or where you could balance relative clauses in separate independent clauses?

CHAPTER 7

Noun Clauses

What Noun Clauses Look Like

1. **That power is the greatest aphrodisiac** was a favorite maxim of former Secretary of State Henry Kissinger.
2. It is possible **that too much cleanliness can leave our immune systems insufficiently challenged.**
3. Some people wonder **whether society is prepared for the coming advances in genetics.**
4. I have not been told yet **if I am a candidate for the job.**
5. A major question for archaeologists is **why the Mayan civilization disappeared.**
6. Owners of SUVs seem not to worry about **what they will do in the next gasoline crisis.**
7. Octavio's discovery **that his roommate had been stealing from him** came as a big shock.

How Grammarians Describe Noun Clauses

If you start a sentence with *I know . . .* , you need a direct object to complete it. This direct object could be a noun phrase such as *your cousin.* It could also be a noun clause such as *that your cousin is honest.* **Noun clauses** are dependent clauses that can go where noun phrases go in sentences; they perform the same sentence functions as noun phrases. They can be subjects, direct objects, objects of the preposition, and so forth. Figure 7.1 gives you a review of these sentence functions and the names for them. If you want to know a bit more about a function, you can look it up in the glossary.

There are two important exceptions to the rule that noun clauses go where noun phrases go in sentences. Unlike noun phrases, noun clauses can function as *delayed* subjects and *delayed* direct objects. In such cases, the normal place of the subject is occupied by *it* functioning as an **expletive,** a word that carries no meaning but merely fills a slot for something that is out of its normal slot. In the following two examples, the subject is the same; it is merely delayed in the second sentence.

Noun clause as subject:	**That Tracy balances the checkbook in that family** is a good thing!
Noun clause as delayed subject:	*It* is a good thing **that Tracy balances the checkbook in that family!**

In the following example, *it* functions as an expletive in the direct object slot; the actual direct object, a noun clause, is delayed.

Noun clause as delayed direct object:	Cameron considered *it* funny **that he should be invited to Julie's wedding.**

Like all dependent clauses, noun clauses are introduced by words that signal that the clause is dependent. Many noun clauses are introduced by the subordinating conjunctions *that, whether,* and *if.* Sometimes *that* is omitted—*I know [that]* ***Kent is loyal***—but in writing it is safer to put the *that* in. Noun clauses may also be introduced by other words such as *why, what, whatever, how,* and *whoever.* Rather than just joining the noun clause to another clause as the conjunctions do, these words perform their own functions within the noun clause. For example, in the next sentence, *whoever* both introduces the noun clause and functions as its subject.

Two free tickets will be given to **whoever calls in first.**

FIGURE 7.1

Sentence Functions Performed by Noun Phrases and Noun Clauses

Sentence function	Noun phrase	Noun clause
Subject	**His lateness** says something about him.	**That he is late** says something about him.
Direct object	Ty believes **her teachers.**	Ty believes **that her teachers are correct.**
Subject complement	My fear is **my problem.**	My fear is **that I may fall.**
Object of preposition	They argued over **money.**	They argued over **who would inherit what.**
Appositive	My friend **Meg** is well known.	The fact **that bats are mammals** is well known.

HOW NOUN CLAUSES ARE PUNCTUATED

Noun clauses are typically not set off by any kind of punctuation. This is because they function as basic sentence elements such as subjects and direct objects, which are not set off from other basic sentence elements. Just as in the sentence *Arthur was very skillful* you do not use a comma after the subject *Arthur,* so you do not use a comma after the subject *Whoever broke into my car last night* in the sentence

Whoever broke into my car last night was very skillful.

When the noun clause is long, you may be tempted to follow it with a comma in order to give your reader a little pause, but this is a mistake. Where a noun clause is so long as to make the sentence seem top heavy, the best thing to do is to use the expletive *it* and make the noun clause a delayed subject. In neither case, however, do you use a comma.

That the kind of communism practiced in the former Soviet Union did not provide for the needs of the vast majority of the population is now fairly obvious to most unbiased observers.

It is now fairly obvious to most unbiased observers **that the kind of communism practiced in the former Soviet Union did not provide for the needs of the vast majority of the population.**

The only noun clause that is ever set off from the rest of the sentence by punctuation is the rare nonrestrictive appositive (see chapter 3). This is usually set off by dashes.

The Immigration and Naturalization Service's position—**that a child could not ask for asylum**—was upheld by the Supreme Court.

What You Can Do with Noun Clauses

1. Express an Idea about an Idea

Because they contain subjects, verbs, and modifiers, noun clauses can express whole ideas just as sentences can. Because the clauses themselves can be the subjects and objects of sentences, they can have ideas expressed about them.

Idea: Violence on television can lead to violent behavior.
Idea: This has been demonstrated by scientific studies.
⇓
That violence on television can lead to violent behavior has been demonstrated by scientific studies.

The more common pattern, in which a noun clause functions as a delayed subject, permits you to plant in advance the viewpoint you want your reader to take of the idea in the noun clause. We often use this structure to establish views or attitudes first and then to express what they are about.

It is a sign of the remarkable success of Federal Express **that "fedex" has become a verb in American English.**
It was a stroke of good luck **that we found the mountain cave just before the snow started falling heavily.**

In her 1813 novel, *Pride and Prejudice,* Jane Austen used the structure for one of the most famous (and most tongue-in-cheek) opening sentences in British literature.

"It is a truth universally acknowledged **that a single man in possession of a good fortune must be in want of a wife.**" (Jane Austen, *Pride and Prejudice,* New York: New American Library, 1980, 5.)

A common pattern in academic writing uses a noun clause as an appositive to a word such as *fact, evidence, belief,* and *theory.*

Experts now dismiss the *belief* **that Stone Age people clothed themselves in animal pelts.** Subtle but intricate patterns on Stone Age figurines support the *theory* **that Stone Age people had the ability to weave plant fibers into cloth.**

Another useful pattern in academic writing, when you are reporting the views of other people, uses a noun clause as a delayed direct object.

Some researchers now consider *it* probable **that Mayan civilization collapsed following a severe drought in the southern Yucatan Peninsula.**

2. Refer to Someone or Something Indefinite

Noun clauses beginning with indefinite pronouns such as *who, whoever, whom, whomever, what,* and *whatever* are useful when you want to refer not to a particular person or thing but to something generalized.

You are **what you eat.**
The teacher could not imagine **who would leave a thumbtack on his chair.**

3. Replace Some Relative Clauses

This can save words and achieve greater directness. It is most useful when the relative clause is referring to someone or something unknown.

Relative clause: The person **who said Professor Stapleton is easy** must not have taken one of his tests.

Noun clause: **Whoever said Professor Stapleton is easy** must not have taken one of his tests.

Relative clause: Frederick was a bureaucrat who could not imagine doing anything except that **which was set forth in written regulations.**

Noun clause: Frederick was a bureaucrat who could not imagine doing anything except **what was set forth in written regulations.**

4. Choose between Direct and Indirect Quotation

When you want to report on what somebody else has said or written, you can quote directly or indirectly. When a quotation, direct or indirect, follows a verb such as *say, declare,* and *ask,* it is a noun clause functioning as the direct object of the verb. The indirect quotation is introduced by *that.*

Direct quotation: Dr. Alvin Poussaint asks, **"If you have a mental process that leads some people to commit genocide, how can you not think that's a mental disorder?"**

Indirect quotation: Dr. Alvin Poussaint believes **that a mental process that leads some people to commit genocide must be classified as a mental disorder.**

This choice permits you to save direct quotation for cases where the precise words matter.

> Dr. Nathaniel Becker does not believe **that therapists have to get to the root of phobias to cure them.** He quips, **"There is more to the surface than meets the eye."**

5. Create Coordination and Parallelism

It is easy to signal coordination among noun clauses by repeating the conjunctions or other words they start with.

> "We have always known **that heedless self-interest was bad morals;** we know now **that it is bad economics.**" (Franklin D. Roosevelt, Second Inaugural Address, January 20, 1937.)

> Don't watch **what he says;** watch **what he does.**

> Generosity should be measured not by **how much a person gives** but by **how much sacrifice the gift entails.**

However, noun clauses do not have to begin with the same word in order to be parallel.

> I was bothered not by **what you said** but by **how you said it.**

Figure 7.2
Punctuating Noun Clauses

No punctuation is used to join most noun clauses to independent clauses.

That a genetically altered tomato may contain a gene from something as different as a fish makes some people nervous.
The fact **that I never remember our wedding anniversary but never forget a golf date** has no special significance whatsoever.

Exercises

A. Practicing Sentence Combining

Combine each group of sentences into one sentence that uses at least one noun clause. The starred clause should be the independent clause. The noun clause should start with the word in parentheses; two words in parentheses mean that there should be two noun clauses. If the combination is a compound sentence, we suggest a coordinating conjunction in brackets.

Examples

He promises something.
He delivers something.
*One may not be the same as the other. (what)

What he promises may not be the same as what he delivers.

Money plays too large a role in American politics.
*Most observers think this. (that)

What should we do about it?
*[, but] They don't know this. (what)

Most observers think that money plays too large a role in American politics, but they don't know what to do about it.

1. You earn something.
You spend something.
*One should depend on the other. (what, what)

2. Something must be done about health care costs.
   *Everybody agrees on this. (that)
   How should the problem be attacked?
   *[, but] Nobody agrees on this. (how)

3. How do you phrase something?
   How do people react to it?
   *One thing has everything to do with the other thing. (how, how)

4. Will the next president be a Republican?
   Will the next president be a Democrat?
   *Analysts cannot yet predict this. (whether)

5. She was not telling the truth.
   *This emerged only after a careful piecing together of stories from many people who were intimately acquainted with the situation and the people involved. (that)

6. Someone will leave the room last.
   *This someone should turn off the lights. (whoever)

7. *There was a time when a woman's status was determined by something. (whom)
   To whom was she attached?

8. *Before making your statement, please tell us these things. (where, how long, whom)
   Where do you live?
   How long have you lived there?
   Whom do you live with?

9. *Some successful people are slow to admit something. (how much, where, when, whom)
   How much of their success do they owe to certain things?
   These things include where they were born.
   These things include when they were born.
   These things include the people to whom they happened to be born.

10. Is the new policy working?
    Is the new policy not working?
    *It will be a long time before we can tell. (whether)

11. Is *Beloved* Toni Morrison's best novel or not?
    *Some people argue about this. (whether)

12. It is an extraordinary book.
    *Of that there is no doubt. (that)
13. *It concerns Sethe, a runaway slave whose house in Cincinnati is haunted by a ghost that drives off people. (whoever)
    It drives off any people who come near.
14. *One thing soon becomes clear. (that)
    The ghost is that of Sethe's dead daughter, Beloved.
15. *Beloved materializes into a young woman who one day appears and gradually comes between Sethe and something. (what)
    That is the little sanity that still exists in Sethe's life.
16. *She drives off Paul D., who loves Sethe but cannot understand something. (why)
    Why does Sethe do whatever Beloved demands?
17. *After her escape from slavery, Sethe had resolved something. (that)
    None of her children would ever be recaptured into slavery.
18. *This determination led her into an act. (what)
    This act must be called terrible.
19. Was it ultimately right or wrong?
    *This is something that readers must decide for themselves. (whether)
20. How will they decide?
    *This may be affected by what the book teaches them about something.
    How did a slave woman experience slavery? (how, how)

B. Writing Your Own Noun Clauses

1. Write five of your own sentences that use noun clauses as subjects. (Example: *That Jeremy was lying was obvious to everyone.*)
2. Write five of your own sentences that use noun clauses as delayed subjects. (Example: *It is astounding that most people are still indifferent to global warming.*)
3. Write five of your own sentences that use noun clauses as direct objects. (Example: *I believe that kindness is more important than brilliance.*)

C. Noun Clauses in Published Writing

Here is a passage by writer Steven Pinker. Locate the noun clauses in the passage and comment on their use. How might the same information be conveyed without noun clauses? Compare the effects of other possible phrasings with the effect of the original.

> As we shall see in this chapter, there is no scientific evidence that languages dramatically shape their speakers' way of thinking. But I want to do more than review the unintentionally comical history of attempts to prove that they do. The idea that language shapes thinking seemed plausible when scientists were in the dark about how thinking works, or even how we should study it. Now that cognitive scientists know how we should think about thinking there is less temptation to equate it with language just because words are more palpable than thoughts. By understanding why linguistic determinism is wrong, we will be in a better position to understand how language itself works when we turn to it in the next chapters.
>
> Steven Pinker, *The Language Instinct*
> (New York: HarperPerennial, 1995), 59.

D. Combining in Context

Rewrite the following paragraphs, making effective use of noun clauses. Create coordinated clauses where these would be effective.

1. Children should be immunized against the worst childhood diseases. This is accepted by most Americans today. Dramatic statistics demonstrate the success of immunization efforts in the United States. In 1934, there were approximately 2.5 million cases of whooping cough; in 1987 there were approximately 5,000. In 1952, there were approximately 21 thousand cases of polio; in 1997 there were zero. But this success is having an ironic and alarming result. Some people are beginning to wonder. Are immunizations still necessary or desirable? These people point to a fact. Some vaccines do cause reactions. A small number of these reactions can be severe. However, both the risk and the consequences of a child's contracting diphtheria, tetanus, whooping cough, or polio are much greater than the risks and consequences of reaction to the vaccines. Moreover, the chance that some disease will re-emerge as a real

threat increases with each person who does not get immunized against it. Do you vaccinate your child or not? Your answer can determine more than what happens to your child. What happens to many other children, too? Your answer can determine that. There are people who have cared for a very sick child. Anybody who has done that would not risk creating more sick children.

2. German could replace English as the language of the United States. This seems highly unlikely today. But in the 1830s and 1840s there were people who feared that it could. They pointed to several facts. German immigrants were pouring into this country. They were continuing to speak German among themselves. States had begun passing laws permitting German to be taught in public schools. Pennsylvania and Wisconsin even permitted schools in which all instruction was in German. We should keep this in mind when we discuss the current "threat" posed by Spanish in the United States. Some people see it as this. Such people point to the large numbers of Spanish-speaking immigrants and their insistence on speaking Spanish among themselves. They also point to bilingual education. Does bilingual education help or hinder immigrant children in learning English? This may be debated. Is bilingual education a threat to the unity of the United States? Even this may be debated. But those who oppose such education cannot claim one thing. Past generations of immigrant children did not all have to "sink or swim" in English. Many received schooling in their native languages—languages that many of their present-day descendants do not know a word of!

E. Revising Your Writing for Style

Choose a piece of your own writing and revise it using noun clauses where these would be effective. Consider the following questions when you think about revising.

1. Are there places where you can efficiently join two ideas by putting one in a noun clause?
2. Are there places where you can save words and gain directness by using a noun clause to refer to an indefinite someone or something or to replace a relative clause construction?

3. Are there direct quotations that could just as easily be indirect quotations, so that you can reserve direct quotations for passages where the original language matters?
4. Are there parallel ideas that could be brought more closely together through coordinate noun clauses?

CHAPTER 8

ADVERB CLAUSES

WHAT ADVERB CLAUSES LOOK LIKE

1. Jason snores **when he sleeps.**
2. **Although I was born in Jersey City,** I call myself a New Yorker.
3. Thelma is the kind of person who, when the time runs out on her parking meter, **dutifully moves her car rather than feeding the meter.**
4. In Chaucer's time, books were expensive **because each one had to be copied manually.**
5. My daughter is **as** athletic **as my son is musical.**
6. Gina worked **so** quickly **that she was finished before lunchtime.**
7. International cartels are harder to fight **than national monopolies are.**
8. **When Max starts looking before 11:00 A.M., when he stops waiting a day or two to answer telephone messages, and when he logs on to *jobs@work.com* before he logs on to *games@play.com***—then I'll believe he is serious about finding a job.

How Grammarians Describe Adverb Clauses

Adverb clauses are dependent clauses that do what adverbs do: they principally modify verbs. They also modify adjectives and other adverbs. Adverb clauses commonly add information related to "adverb questions": when?; why?; how?; how much?; under what condition?; and to what degree? In the first example of this chapter—*Jason snores **when he sleeps***—the adverb clause in boldface tells us *when.* You could easily think of clauses to answer the other questions: *because he has blocked sinuses* (why), *as though he were croaking in his sleep* (how), and so forth.

Adverb clauses are introduced by **subordinating conjunctions.** Because there is a long list of these, grammarians often divide them into categories according to the kind of information they add to a sentence (see figure 8.1). It is not necessary to think much about these categories; most native speakers use the subordinating conjunctions unconsciously.

Just as there are correlative coordinating conjunctions (see chapter 5), there are **subordinating correlative conjunctions.** In some cases, one of them introduces the main clause and one the adverb clause; in each of the following examples, the adverb clause comes first.

> ***If* his story is true,** ***then*** her story is false.
> ***No sooner* does Bruce begin a new job** ***than*** he begins to get restless in it.

In other cases, an adverb clause modifies an adverbial in the main clause such as *so* or *as.*

> Shakespeare's Rosalind is ***as*** masterful ***as* she is vulnerable.**
> My dog sleeps ***so*** soundly ***that* he never heard the burglars.**

In speaking, we might say *The lake was so beautiful.* In writing, however, the *so* is usually modified by an adverb clause: *The lake was* **so** *beautiful* ***that we camped right there.*** Note that this use of *so . . . that* differs from the *so that* used to indicate result.

> Ruth had privately won each committee member to her point of view, **so that** the public meeting went very smoothly.

Adverb clauses may be **elliptical;** that is, certain grammatically necessary words may be omitted as understood.

FIGURE 8.1
Subordinating Conjunctions That Introduce Adverb Clauses

Time:	when, whenever, before, as, just as, after, once, as long as, as soon as, since, until, till, while, now that
Concession:	though, although, even though, if, while, whereas
Condition:	if, unless, on condition that, provided that, in case, as long as, as soon as
Cause:	because, since, as, as long as, inasmuch as
Result:	so that, so . . . that, such . . . that
Purpose:	so, so that, in order that, that, lest
Comparison:	than, as, just as, as if, as . . . as, so . . . as, as if

(*Note:* Especially for spoken English, *like* is beginning to be admitted to this list, as in *He looked* ***like*** *he was lying.*

Manner:	as, as if, as though
Place:	where, wherever

When [Brian is] watching television, Brian hears nothing I say to him.

Although [Karla is] used to rainy weather, Karla finds it depressing this year.

As these examples show, the words omitted from an elliptical adverb clause may include the subject. In such cases, the understood subject must be the same as the subject of the main clause (in the examples, *Brian* and *Brian, Karla* and *Karla*).

When adverb clauses modify verbs (the majority of cases) they are usually movable within a sentence; they can be placed before the main clause, in the middle of it, or after it as long as there is a clear connection to what they modify.

Even though he works harder than his co-workers, Grant never complains.

Grant, **even though he works harder than his co-workers,** never complains.

Grant never complains **even though he works harder than his coworkers.**

When an adverb clause modifies an adjective or an adverb, it usually comes right after the word it modifies. In the following example, the adverb clause modifies the adjective *glad.*

Both sides in the negotiations were glad **that they had reached agreement.**

How Adverb Clauses Are Punctuated

Adverb clauses that come before the main clause are always set off by commas. These are usually right at the beginning of a sentence, and they modify the verb in the main clause.

Before cigarette advertising was banned from U.S. television, tobacco companies were the main sponsors of sports newscasts.

When adverb clauses modifying the verb occur at the end of a sentence they are usually not set off by commas.

We cook vegetarian food **when Nancy stays at our house.**

Jeff is headed for debt trouble: he uses credit cards **as though they were free money.**

Adverb clauses modifying adjectives and adverbs are not set off by commas.

The Chairman of the Federal Reserve is afraid **that low unemployment will cause inflation.**

The current run of national prosperity has lasted longer **than most people had expected.**

What You Can Do with Adverb Clauses

1. Show Relations Concisely

The subordinating conjunctions that introduce adverb clauses can concisely relate ideas or information that might otherwise require separate sentences or wordy constructions.

Original: I try to exercise every day. The reason for this is that otherwise I get depressed.

Revision: I try to exercise every day **because otherwise I get depressed.**

Original: New cars depreciate in value very fast. However, some economists think they may still be better deals in the long run.

Revision: **Even though new cars depreciate in value very fast,** some economists think they may still be better deals in the long run.

Elliptical clauses are of course especially concise. In the following example, the revision omits both a subject and a verb.

Original: I am in favor of regulating development in rural areas. However, I cannot support your proposal as it is worded.

Revision: **Although [I am] in favor of regulating development in rural areas,** I cannot support your proposal as it is worded.

2. Vary Sentence Length and Rhythm

Professional writers typically vary the length and rhythm of their sentences. The movability of many adverb clauses makes them especially useful for this purpose. For example, a sequence of similar sentences beginning with a main clause may be broken up by a sentence introduced by an adverb clause. This usually affects the focus and emphasis, too. In the following example, the final sentence contributes more than variety for variety's sake; it lays special stress on King's youth in relation to the ages of other American leaders who died prematurely.

Many of our most revered historical figures have died before their time. Abraham Lincoln was fifty-six when he was assassinated. Franklin Roosevelt died in office at sixty-three. John F. Kennedy was assassinated at forty-six. **When Martin Luther King Jr. was assassinated,** he was thirty-nine.

Here is Virginia Woolf describing the ideal mother in Victorian England, whom the poet Coventry Patmore had called "The Angel in the House."

"She was intensely sympathetic. She was immensely charming. She was utterly unselfish. She excelled in the difficult arts of family life. She sacrificed herself daily. **If there was chicken,** she took the leg; **if there was a draught,** she sat in it. . . ." (Virginia Woolf, "Professions for Women," in M. H. Abrams, ed., *The Norton Anthology of English Literature,* 6th ed., Vol. 2, New York: Norton, 1993, 1987.)

FIGURE 8.2

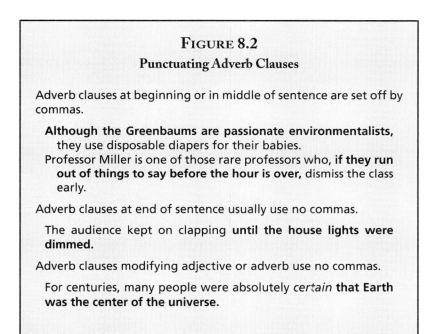

Punctuating Adverb Clauses

Adverb clauses at beginning or in middle of sentence are set off by commas.

> **Although the Greenbaums are passionate environmentalists,** they use disposable diapers for their babies.
>
> Professor Miller is one of those rare professors who, **if they run out of things to say before the hour is over,** dismiss the class early.

Adverb clauses at end of sentence usually use no commas.

> The audience kept on clapping **until the house lights were dimmed.**

Adverb clauses modifying adjective or adverb use no commas.

> For centuries, many people were absolutely *certain* **that Earth was the center of the universe.**

3. Create Coordination and Parallelism

It is easy to signal coordination among adverb clauses by repeating the subordinating conjunctions they start with.

> I used to eat chocolate **because I love it;** now I eat it **because it is good for me.**
>
> **When they were dating,** he was a charmer; **when they got married,** he changed.

Here is a magnificent series of adverb clauses in one sentence from Samuel Johnson's famous letter to Lord Chesterfield in 1749 declining Lord Chesterfield's tardy offer of financial assistance in writing his great *Dictionary of the English Language.*

> "The notice which you have been pleased to take of my labours, had it been early, had been kind; but it has been delayed **till I am indifferent and cannot enjoy it; till I am solitary and cannot impart it; till I am known and do not want it.**" [Samuel Johnson, "Letter to

the Earl of Chesterfield," in *Major British Writers,* ed. G. B. Harrison, (New York: Harcourt, Brace and Company, 1959), 913.]

Series of adverbial clauses can work effectively at the beginning of a sentence, too, by, for instance, keeping the reader waiting to know what will happen until you have laid out all the conditions that must be met before it can happen.

> **If Caitlin can find her shoes, if Bill Jr. can decide on which CDs to bring, if Bill Sr. can tear himself away from his email,** and **if by some miracle I can get just a little help loading up the car,** we may get off on this camping trip yet.

EXERCISES

A. Practicing Sentence Combining

Combine each group of sentences into one sentence that uses at least one adverb clause. Try varying the positions in which you place the adverb clause within the sentence. The starred sentence should be the independent clause. For 1–10, we have also suggested a subordinating conjunction in parentheses; you may want to try a different one (see the list in figure 8.1).

Example

Caetana smiles at me.
Then something happens.
*I forget all my troubles. (as soon as)

As soon as Caetana smiles at me, I forget all my troubles.
When Caetana smiles at me, I forget all my troubles.
I forget all my troubles whenever Caetana smiles at me.

1. *You would be queen. (if)
   But something would have to happen first.
   I would have to be king.
2. *The United States has moved toward diplomatic relations with Vietnam. (although)
   Some Vietnamese Americans have been quite unhappy about this.

3. *Will you love me in December? (as)
   Will you love me in the same way that you do in May?
4. Many Americans think of Chief Joseph as a great military leader.
   *His role was actually to keep the men, women, and children of his band together during their attempted flight to Canada. (although)
5. *The tough get going. (when)
   The going gets tough.
6. *Lord Chesterfield kept Samuel Johnson waiting a long time. (while)
   During that time, Lord Chesterfield talked to someone Johnson despised.
7. *Howard is the kind of person who tells you about every ache and pain he has had in the past year. (when)
   He does this at those times when you ask how he is.
8. Leaders surround themselves with people who are afraid to tell them the truth.
   This happens even at times when they are desperately wrong.
   *In such a case, the leaders are bound to make enormous mistakes. (if)
9. *A woman needs a man. (as/like)
   This need is similar to that of a fish for a bicycle.
10. Does Sergio think he is the only one who can do it?
    Does Sergio think that nobody else can do anything right?
    Does Sergio want to do all the work himself?
    *Then let him! (if)
11. *The witches agree among themselves to meet Macbeth at a certain time.
    At that time, the hurly-burly will be done.
    At that time, the battle will be lost and won.
12. The witches plant in Macbeth's head the idea that he could be king.
    *Then this idea begins to take hold of him.
    This happens in spite of the fact that the idea seems impossible.
13. Macbeth likes the idea of his being king.
    *Lady Macbeth likes it even more.
14. They plan to murder the good, meek King Duncan.
    *Immediately after this, Macbeth begins to waver in his resolve.
    Lady Macbeth had feared he would waver in his resolve.

15. Macbeth is wavering.
    *But Lady Macbeth is equally as determined, and so she takes the lead.
16. Macbeth does the actual killing.
    *After that, Lady Macbeth says that she would even have done the actual killing herself on one condition.
    The condition is that Duncan had not resembled her father as he slept.
17. *Macbeth gets stronger and crueler.
    Lady Macbeth gets weaker and more conscience-stricken.
    This happens as the play proceeds.
18. *But Macbeth sleeps no more.
    A voice had predicted this.
    He sleeps no more for reasons.
    One reason, among other things, is that he is so busy killing anybody he suspects of suspecting him.
19. *In Shakespeare's world, not sleeping goes against nature.
    In Shakespeare's world, killing a king goes against nature.
20. Macbeth says that life is "a tale/Told by an idiot, full of sound and fury/Signifying nothing."
    *He is expressing his state of mind, not Shakespeare's view of life.

B. Writing Your Own Adverb Clauses

1. Write five sentences that open with an adverb clause; use a different subordinating conjunction for each one. (Example: *After the pilots had brought the plane down safely, the passengers broke into applause.*)
2. Write five sentences that end with an adverb clause; use a different subordinating conjunction for each one. (Example: *The college has to keep spending money on current technology because outdated technology is useless.*)
3. Write two sentences that contain elliptical adverb clauses. (Example: *When told that the guards had seen a ghost, Horatio is characteristically skeptical.*)

C. Adverb Clauses in Published Writing

Here is a passage by writer Timothy Ferris. Locate the adverb clauses in the passage and comment on their use. How might the same information be conveyed without adverb clauses? Compare the effects of other possible phrasings with the effect of the original.

> When a star runs out of fuel, it can become unstable and explode, spewing much of its substance, now rich in iron and other heavy elements, into space. As time passes, this expanding bubble of gas is intermixed with passing interstellar clouds. The sun and its planets congealed from such a cloud. Time passed, human beings appeared, miners in the north of England dug the iron from the earth, and ironmongers pounded it into nails that longshoremen loaded in barrels into the holds of H.M.S. *Endeavor.* Off the nails went to Tahiti, continuing a journey that had begun in the bowels of stars that died before the sun was born. The nails that [Captain] Cook's men traded with the Tahitian dancing girls, while on an expedition to measure the distance of the sun, were, themselves, the shards of ancient suns.
>
> Timothy Ferris, *Coming of Age in the Milky Way* (New York: Anchor, 1988), 140–141.

D. Combining in Context

Rewrite the following paragraphs, making effective use of adverb clauses. Pay special attention to paragraph coherence. Look for places where paragraph coherence can be improved if you change an independent clause to an adverb clause. Create coordinated clauses where these would be effective.

1. For many families, childcare is a more complicated issue today than it was in an earlier day. Then, many mothers stayed home with their children. Today, many mothers work outside the home. For some, the reason is that they have to; for others, the reason is that they want to. Forty hours of day care per week cost about $1000 per month in Seattle in 1999. Sometimes, families can afford to pay that. Then they must still find appropriate day care. Sometimes they cannot afford it. Then they must seek other solutions. Some turn to grandparents. Childcare by grandparents has always been a feature of life for low-income families. It is increasingly a feature of middle-income life, too. Many families are finding that there must be collaboration among different branches and different generations. This is a condition of having children.
2. Maybe you look for many turns of event in a play. In that case, little seems to happen in Aeschylus's *Agamemnon.* Agamemnon comes home

from the Trojan War and is murdered by his wife, Clytemnestra. This event springs from a number of other events that happened at an earlier time—before the play began. Starting with his great-grandfather, Tantalus, Agamemnon's family history is full of parents murdering children and children murdering parents. Agamemnon himself sacrificed his daughter Iphigenia to the gods. His reason for doing this was that he would gain their help in the Trojan War. The play even suggests that his victories in the war involved acts of killing for which the gods will exact revenge. The play is an extended reflection on how there is no end to pain and destruction in human affairs. How long this goes on is determined by how long people cling to the idea of revenge. In the two plays that follow *Agamemnon*—*The Libation Bearers* (in which Agamemnon's son, Orestes, avenges his father's death by killing his mother) and *The Eumenides*—Aeschylus shows the Greeks finally breaking the cycle of revenge. They do this; then they move toward civil society.

E. Revising Your Writing for Style

Choose a piece of your own writing and revise it using adverb clauses where these would be effective. Consider the following questions when you think about revising.

1. Are there places where you can use adverb clauses to concisely show relations among ideas or information?
2. Are there places where you could use adverb clauses to achieve greater variety of sentence length and rhythm?
3. Are there places where you could effectively use a pair or a series of coordinated adverb clauses?

CHAPTER 9

GERUND PHRASES

WHAT GERUND PHRASES LOOK LIKE

1. **Declaring war** has always been a prerogative of Congress.
2. Some experts advocate **letting forest fires burn unchecked unless they pose a direct danger to human life and property.**
3. Don's favorite activities are **reaching for potato chips** and **pressing the remote.**
4. My most stressful memory is of **having been chased by a Rottweiler.**
5. My job, **parking cars at the Sheraton,** gives me a chance to drive many fancy models.
6. Some people credit Edward de Vere with **having written the plays attributed to William Shakespeare.**
7. "Even **voting for the right** is **doing nothing for it.** It is **merely expressing to men feebly your desire that it should prevail.**" Henry David Thoreau, "Civil Disobedience" (1848).

HOW GRAMMARIANS DESCRIBE GERUND PHRASES

Gerunds are the first of three verbals we look at in this book. **Verbals** are words formed from verbs but functioning as something else in sentences. That gerunds are formed from verbs accounts for the fact that every gerund either ends in *-ing* (*playing, climbing*) or has auxiliaries that end in *-ing* (*being played, having climbed*).

Gerunds function in sentences as nouns. They can be subjects, direct objects, and so forth (see figure 9.1). For instance, it should not be hard for you to think of a gerund that could fill the subject slot in the following example.

> ____________________ is a strenuous activity.

While they function as nouns, gerunds retain some verb qualities, such as the ability to take complements and adverbial modifiers. When they do, they expand into **gerund phrases.** For example, *climbing* can take the direct object *mountains* to become the gerund phrase *climbing mountains.* It could expand even more with adverbial modifiers to become *climbing mountains in hot weather,* and *mountains* could get its own modifier, such as *high.* The subject of the sentence is now the whole phrase.

> **Climbing high mountains in hot weather** is strenuous.

The example sentences that open this chapter include some fairly long and elaborate gerund phrases.

HOW GERUND PHRASES ARE PUNCTUATED

Gerund phrases are punctuated pretty much in the same way they would be punctuated if they were single nouns performing the same sentence functions. That means that no punctuation is used between most gerunds and the other sentence elements; we do not set subjects off from verbs or verbs off from complements like direct objects. Just as in the sentence *Basketball requires stamina* there is no comma between the subject *Basketball* and the verb *requires,* so also there is no comma if *Basketball* is replaced by a gerund phrase such as *Playing basketball.*

> **Playing basketball** requires stamina.

FIGURE 9.1
Sentence Functions Performed by Gerund Phrases

Sentence function	Gerund phrase
Subject	**Censoring rap lyrics** is not the answer to our moral problems.
Direct object	The law forbids **putting hazardous materials in the garbage.**
Indirect object	You might give **regular studying** a try.
Subject complement	Ricardo's mistake was **considering Anya trustworthy.**
Object of preposition	The boss raised morale by **working alongside the employees.**
Appositive	Dale's hobby, **restoring old clocks**, became a nice little business.

This is true even if that gerund phrase happens to be rather lengthy.

> **Playing full-court basketball against energetic sixteen-year-olds on a hot day** requires stamina.

Gerunds functioning as appositives are generally nonrestrictive and, like other nonrestrictive noun appositives, are set off by commas or, if they occur at the end of a sentence, sometimes by a colon (see chapter 3).

> Clarence's method of persuasion, **speaking in an increasingly strident voice,** was seldom successful.
> He always failed at the rhetorician's most important task: **persuading his audience that he is reasonable.**

Of course, because gerund phrases can include such elements as complements and modifiers, they can have internal punctuation.

> Sven started the conflict by **making hostile, unprovoked remarks to Stan, his rival for Vera's attentions.**

WHAT YOU CAN DO WITH GERUND PHRASES

1. Create Verb Power in Noun Slots

Because they are made from verbs, gerunds can bring action into parts of a sentence normally filled by nouns or noun substitutes. And because gerund phrases can include their own complements and modifiers, you can get much of the power and information of a verb in a noun slot and still have a real verb in the verb slot. You can use this power to relate one action to another.

> **Riding in a car for a long time** makes me sick.

Consider how much more directly this sentence shows cause than a sentence that uses an adverb clause to suggest the same thing: *Whenever I ride in a car for a long time, I get sick.* The gerund version directly relates the *riding* to the *makes me sick.* In the following example, the gerund puts the focus directly on the action that got Microsoft into trouble.

> **Bundling Windows 98 with Microsoft Explorer** got Microsoft into big trouble.

2. Focus on the Action

Sometimes it is the action, not the doer of the action, that is important; sometimes the doer is everybody in general. Gerund phrases convey this efficiently.

> **Charging a lot more for parking** may encourage more use of public transit.
>
> Some experts advocate **letting forest fires burn unchecked unless they pose a direct danger to human life and property.**

3. Connect an Action to Its Doer

Sometimes you want to focus on an action, but still connect it to the doer. You can do this by having a possessive determiner in front of the gerund phrase.

> David's **actually coming to the meeting** made all the difference.

This says the same thing as the compound sentence *David actually came to the meeting, and this made all the difference.* But the sentence with the gerund

FIGURE 9.2

Punctuating Gerund Phrases

No punctuation is used between most gerund phrases and other sentence elements.

> **Picking huckleberries in the August heat** exhausts me.
>
> I do love **eating my dad's special huckleberry pie.**

Gerund phrases functioning as nonrestrictive appositives are set off by commas.

> Eric's job, **recruiting computer scientists for a high-tech company,** is challenging.

phrase is not only two words shorter; it is more intensely focused and direct in linking *coming* to *made all the difference. David* is important here and gets mentioned, but his *coming* is even more important and gets the prime subject slot in the sentence. Similarly in the next example, it is not Jules but a specific action by Jules that did the hurting, although Jules certainly needs to be mentioned.

> I expect an apology from Jules. His **calling me a zealot** hurt my feelings.

4. Borrow the Subject of an Independent Clause

You can put another action by the subject of an independent clause in a gerund phrase functioning as the object of a preposition.

> After **talking to the counselor,** I considered my problems less serious than I had thought.

This useful construction works only when the subject of the gerund phrase is the same as the subject of the main clause. When the subject is different, the gerund phrase is improperly connected to the main clause.

> ∅After talking to the counselor, my problems seemed less serious than I had thought.

Such an improperly connected phrase is called a **dangling modifier.** We deal with dangling modifiers at greater length in chapter 10.

5. Create Coordination and Parallelism

Because of their consistent *-ing* endings and use in particular patterns—for instance, gerund plus direct object—gerund phrases lend themselves to parallelism in series and to being balanced on either side of a linking verb.

Our conversation last night went a long way toward **improving communications, resolving differences,** and **cementing our relationship.**
Contradicting our supervisor is like **confronting a bear:** people usually do it only once.
Swimming by yourself is **asking for trouble.**

EXERCISES

A. Practicing Sentence Combining

Combine each set of sentences into a single sentence, using gerund phrases when appropriate. In 1–10, the words in boldface can be replaced by gerund phrases.

Examples

I talk to the passenger next to me.
This helps calm my nerves in an airplane.

Talking to the passenger next to me helps calm my nerves in an airplane.

Harold achieved a very high grade in English by **several methods.**
He worked hard.
He participated energetically in class.
He brought the instructor lots of fine chocolate.

Harold achieved a very high grade in English by working hard, participating energetically in class, and bringing the instructor lots of fine chocolate.

1. One makes mistakes.
   This is often the best way to learn.
2. One learns to write.
   This should not be like **something dangerous.**
   To crawl across a minefield under enemy fire is something dangerous.

3. The authorities received a bomb threat.
   Immediately after **this happened,** they evacuated the building.
4. I oppose my country's participation in this war.
   I am disloyal to my country.
   One thing is not **another thing.**
5. When you are shopping for a bank loan, you can tell which loan costs the least by **a certain method.**
   The method is to compare annual percentage rates (APRs).
6. Valeria is known for **something.**
   She does what she says she will do.
7. You call a novel religious because one of its characters is Jesus.
   You call a novel scientific because one of its characters is Newton.
   One thing is like **another.**
8. Mark is a Nelson.
   This fact seems to have helped him in **something.**
   He has gotten promoted to top management in the Nelson Clothing Company.
9. To declare war is the prerogative of the legislative branch.
   Although the Constitution clearly makes it a prerogative of the legislative branch, U.S. presidents have often gotten around this by **one method.**
   They have sent military forces into action without **a declaration.**
   The declaration is of war.
10. Linguists do not want to be misled by coincidental resemblances between words from two different languages.
    To avoid **this,** linguists examine the evidence extremely carefully before **something.**
    That something is to declare that the languages are related to a common source language.
11. Siddhartha's father tried to keep the young man's thoughts on worldly happiness by a method.
    The method was to surround Siddhartha with unlimited luxury and pleasure.
12. Despite all their efforts, his servants could not prevent something.
    Siddhartha encountered an old man, a sick man, and a corpse.
    He realized that to live for physical pleasure is futile.

13. Siddhartha's long quest for lasting happiness led to something.
He became Buddha, the Awakened One.
14. He had awakened to knowledge.
The knowledge was that the Eightfold Path is the key to something.
This something is to overcome the egoistic, self-seeking desire for separate existence that is the root of human suffering.
15. If one decides to follow the path, it means something.
It means that one adopts a rigorous program of habit formation aimed at something.
The aim is to remake a person completely.
16. After he experienced the Great Awakening, Buddha devoted the rest of his life to something.
He preached his message in public.
He counseled thousands of people in private.
17. He maintained his creativity by a regular pattern.
He withdrew from the world.
He returned to it.
18. He made his enormous impact on people by this.
He had a combination of qualities: extraordinary intellect and infinite compassion.
19. He resisted all attempts to turn him into a god.
He did this by an insistence on the fact that he was fully human.
20. His religion differed from the Hinduism of his day in what it was.
It was devoid of authority, ritual, speculation, and tradition.

B. Writing Your Own Gerund Phrases

1. Write five sentences that use a gerund phrase as a subject. (Example: *Paying taxes is a patriotic duty.*)
2. Write five sentences that use a gerund phrase as a direct object. (Example: *The Olympic Games Committee began requiring drug tests eight years ago.*)
3. Write five sentences that use a gerund phrase as an object of a preposition. (Example: *After winning the lottery, Aaron became confused about what to do with his life.*)

4. Write two sentences that use coordinate, parallel, or balanced gerund phrases. (Example: *Playing with drugs is playing with fire.*)

C. Gerund Phrases in Published Writing

The following is a passage by writer Peter Gleick. Locate the gerund phrases in the passage and comment on their use. How might the same information be conveyed without gerund phrases? Compare the effects of other possible phrasings with the effect of the original.

> I am disappointed about one thing: the decision by Scholastic, publisher of the American edition, to translate the books from "English" into "American." . . . I like to think that our society would not collapse if our children started calling their mothers Mum instead of Mom. And I would hate to think that today's children would be frightened away from an otherwise thrilling book by reading that the hero is wearing a jumper instead of a sweater. . . .
>
> Do we really want children to think that crumpets are the same as English muffins? Frankly, reading about Harry and Hermione eating crumpets during tea is far more interesting to an American than reading about them eating English muffins during a meal.
>
> By protecting our children from an occasional misunderstanding or trip to the dictionary, we are pretending that other cultures are, or should be, the same as ours. By insisting that everything be Americanized, we dumb down our own society rather than enrich it.
>
> Peter H. Gleick, "Harry Potter, Minus a Certain Flavour," *New York Times,* July 10, 2000, A25.

D. Combining in Context

Rewrite the following paragraphs, making effective use of gerund phrases. Create coordinated phrases where these would be effective.

1. Tim had asked Maria out to dinner, and this had been hard enough. Something else took real research: to prepare to impress her at dinner. This involved several things: he had to go to the restaurant in advance, he had to get its dinner menu to study it, and he had to learn the meaning and pronunciation of all those French expressions. That soup *du jour,* for instance. Was *jour* an animal? Maria was vegetarian, though

she ate seafood. What about the eggplant *en croute?* Did that rhyme with "out" or with "hoot"? His roommate suggested something, which was just to stay away from anything with French in it. But his roommate didn't know he had told Maria that, after meeting her, he was thinking of still majoring in computer science but that his minor would be Romance languages. He'd meant it as a joke, but she had seemed so impressed that he was stuck with it. Well, at least he was pretty sure he'd mastered the first word in *crème brûlée.*

2. For years, leaded gasoline was blamed for high atmospheric lead levels in urban areas. The means by which authorities sought to lower these levels was to require that automobile engines burn unleaded gas. New studies now suggest that the authorities should have discouraged people from something else: When people burned garbage they caused more pollution than when they burned leaded gasoline. Researchers examining core samples from the bottom of New York's Central Park Lake have established that the biggest rise in heavy-metal pollutants occurred between 1860 and 1930. This was before the heyday of leaded gasoline; instead, it was the heyday of incinerator construction and use in the New York area. The widespread use of leaded gasoline in the late 1960s and early 1970s added very little to the lead deposits in the lake. So maybe defenders of leaded gas were partly right when they said, "Don't knock it!"

E. Revising Your Writing for Style

Choose a short piece of your own writing—perhaps just three consecutive paragraphs out of a longer piece—and revise it using gerund phrases where these would be effective. Consider the following questions when you think about revising.

1. Are there loose structures and words that don't seem to be doing any real work? Could gerund phrases help eliminate them?
2. Are there places where gerunds could help focus on actions?
3. Where gerund phrases are already in the paragraphs, could others be created near them for effective coordination, parallelism, or balance?

CHAPTER 10

Participle Phrases

What Participle Phrases Look Like

1. **Racing down the stairs,** I collided with the college president.
2. **Breaking the bottle of dye,** I realized that I was wearing my only white shirt.
3. **Broken years ago,** the bicycle remains in a corner of the garage.
4. The wet rocks, **glistening in the sun,** attracted Maria's attention.
5. Toan walked on a path near the lake, **burdened with thoughts of his exams.**
6. The car flipped over after it hit a snowplow **sitting beside the road.**
7. Payton moved the ball slowly down the floor. He seemed to have forgotten that clocks were moving, that he did not have forever to get across the centerline and to get off a shot. Suddenly he broke loose, **bouncing the ball, weaving between the waving arms of the opposition,**

jumping forward, and at the last minute, **passing off to Schrempf,** who made the basket.

HOW GRAMMARIANS DESCRIBE PARTICIPLE PHRASES

Traditionally, **participles** and **participle phrases** (also sometimes called **participial phrases**) have been described as functioning as adjectives in a sentence, modifying nouns or pronouns. Like gerunds, participles are verbals, but they are a little more complicated than gerunds, for they come in two forms, present and past. The present participle is formed just like the gerund by adding *-ing* to a verb, and because it functions like an adjective, it becomes part of a noun phrase (*the **coming** events*). The past participle is formed by adding *-ed* to a regular verb (irregular verbs have irregular past participle forms); it too becomes part of a noun phrase (*the **loaded** gun; the **broken** window*).

When complements and adverbial modifiers are added to participles, participles become participle phrases; the participle is the headword in the participle phrase.

Coming from the southwest, this wind means rain.
Broken in the last storm, the window needs to be replaced.

Participle phrases are often seen as reductions of independent or dependent clauses. So *Coming from the southwest* might come from *This wind is coming from the southwest,* or *which is coming from the southwest.* Generally grammarians see participle phrases as reductions of relative clauses, and therefore consider them adjectival.

Relative clause:	Bob is the man **who is wearing the Hawaiian shirt.**
Participle phrase:	Bob is the man **wearing the Hawaiian shirt.**

But sometimes participle phrases seem to be reduced adverb clauses, and some grammarians see these participle phrases functioning adverbially.

Adverb clause:	**While he was listening to the lecture,** the student fell asleep.
Participle phrase:	**Listening to the lecture,** the student fell asleep.

Understanding that participle phrases can be seen as reductions of clauses can help you avoid the **dangling modifier,** a very common problem. If I begin a sentence *Wanting only peace and quiet,* you expect the subject that follows to be a person or animal, something capable of wanting peace and quiet. If instead, I continue ... *the bus roared down the street,* you will be momentarily confused. The sentence syntax is not working the way that the language-understanding part of the brain expects. The expectation is that a participle phrase at the beginning of a sentence must come from a clause that has the same subject as the subject of the base sentence. If it comes from a clause with a different subject, you have a dangling participle.

Jerome thought about his future.
Jerome entered the employment office.
Thinking about his future, *Jerome* entered the employment office.

Jerome was looking desperately for work.
The *job board* was empty.
∅**Looking desperately for work,** the *job board* was empty.

This same rule also holds true for infinitives and gerunds, but the mistake is less common. It is participles that usually give us problems; we know what we mean, so we do not stop to think about what we have actually said. Historically, the dangling participle has always been around, and in spoken English dangling participles are not unforgivable, but they are best eliminated from written English.

How Participle Phrases Are Punctuated

Punctuating the participle phrase is fairly simple. You have probably noticed that the participle phrase at the beginning of the sentence is always set off with a comma. When a participle phrase comes at the end of the sentence and modifies the subject of the sentence, it too is set off with a comma. Participle phrases that come immediately after the word that they modify are punctuated in the same way as relative clauses. If they are restrictive, they are not set off with commas; if they are nonrestrictive, they are set off with commas. (See chapter 6.)

Beginning of sentence: **Ricocheting off the sides of the polished aluminum tube,** the light intensifies.

End of sentence:	She stopped in the middle of a thought, **realizing that she had just taken the wrong freeway exit.**
Restrictive:	The man **wearing the Hawaiian shirt** is my father.
Nonrestrictive:	Humans, **being bipedal,** often have back problems because of their upright position.

What You Can Do with Participle Phrases

1. Add Focus to Your Writing

As we have already seen, participle phrases can be used to tighten writing; usually that tightening involves more focused, more forceful sentences. Often the force and focus that we create in speech through a louder voice and through body and facial gestures we create in writing through such syntactic structures as the participle phrase. In fact, the participle phrase is used much more frequently in writing than it is in everyday speech.

When the bell rang at noon, I set off for the piazza. I hoped to find romance.

Hearing the noon bell ring, I set off for the piazza, **hoping to find romance.**

2. Create Verb Power in Adjective Slots

In addition to tightening the focus, the participle phrase, because it is made from a verb, adds verb power to the adjective modifier.

David Letterman put his hands in his pockets and walked toward the podium.

Putting his hands in his pockets, David Letterman walked toward the podium.

Even though both of these sentences are the same length, notice the added focus on the actions of both *putting* and *walked* in the second sentence. *Walked* is clearly the verb of focus because it is in the independent clause, but *putting* also gets focus because it is now the first word of the sentence. One thing that is lost is a clear sense of when *putting* occurs. Both *before* and *while* are possible interpretations of the participle phrase; so if clarity about the sequence of events is needed, an independent clause, an adverb clause, or a compound verb might be necessary.

3. Add Detail to Your Writing

Also notice that in the previous example, *putting his hands in his pockets* is a detail added to the general picture: *David Letterman walked to the podium.* Adding detail is one of the most important functions of a participle phrase, and adding detail almost invariably improves your writing.

> The kitten played with the ball of yarn, **swatting at it, nudging it across the floor,** and **finally unraveling a long piece.**
>
> "She read on, lost, **drowsing, flicking minute creatures from the pages, scratching mechanically at her leg,** where the grass pricked her." [Nadine Gordimer, "The Kindest Thing to Do," in *Literature and Its Writers: An Introduction to Fiction, Poetry, and Drama,* ed. Ann Charters (Boston: Bedford Books, 1997), 260.]

4. Indicate Cause

Indicating cause is another possible function of the participle phrase; usually when the participle phrase indicates cause, it comes before the base sentence, which contains the effect clause.

> **Hearing that the Nez Perce had escaped,** General Howard was furious.

It is also possible, however, for the phrase to come after the subject when cause is indicated.

> General Howard, **hearing that the Nez Perce had escaped,** was furious.

The cause can also come after the effect in some sentences, but notice that the sentence loses some of the sense of cause and effect and might be interpreted as indicating simultaneity rather than cause and effect.

> Vu examined his cat, **checking for fleas.**

5. Add Energy to a Sentence

As we have said, the participle phrase adds energy to a sentence because of its verb qualities. The present participle phrase also adds energy to a sentence because it ends in an unaccented syllable—*-ing*. Because English is a stress language, sentences typically end on a stressed rather than on an

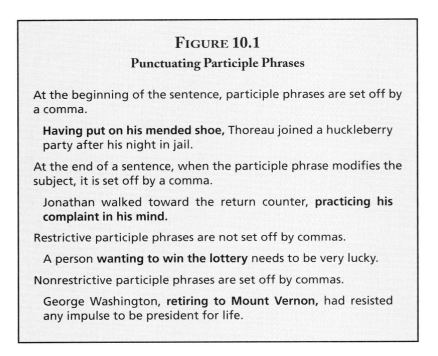

FIGURE 10.1
Punctuating Participle Phrases

At the beginning of the sentence, participle phrases are set off by a comma.

> **Having put on his mended shoe,** Thoreau joined a huckleberry party after his night in jail.

At the end of a sentence, when the participle phrase modifies the subject, it is set off by a comma.

> Jonathan walked toward the return counter, **practicing his complaint in his mind.**

Restrictive participle phrases are not set off by commas.

> A person **wanting to win the lottery** needs to be very lucky.

Nonrestrictive participle phrases are set off by commas.

> George Washington, **retiring to Mount Vernon,** had resisted any impulse to be president for life.

unstressed syllable. The sentence needs a place to land, so it keeps rushing on until it finds that landing place. Therefore, present participle phrases are particularly good for describing scenes that contain a lot of action. They are not so good for describing more passive or inactive situations

> **Streaking down the freeway, cutting in and out of traffic,** the ambulance raced for the hospital.

6. Create Coordination and Parallelism

Notice also in the last example that two or more participle phrases can be used in a series; in this case, the series increases the sense of speed. Participle phrases are very effective in a series; when we want to stress action, a series of present participle phrases can produce an almost breakneck speed in the sentence (see sentence 7 at the beginning of this chapter). Present and past participle phrases can be mixed in a series, and they can be combined with adjective phrases; the phrases can also be balanced both before and after a main clause.

The children raced toward the beach, **testing the icy water, splashing one another, screaming with delight.**

Huddled together for warmth, squeaking from time to time, the cubs awaited the return of their mother.

Rolling up their pant legs, ready for high water, the girls waited for the next breaker.

Dressed in her band uniform, Jeanine walked toward the parade ground, **holding her new flute carefully.**

And, of course, the participle phrases can be balanced between sentences to create parallelism between sentences also.

The male, **demonstrating his interest,** beats his chest. The female, **indicating her acquiescence,** remains motionless.

Exercises

A. Practicing Sentence Combining

Combine each of the following pairs into one sentence that uses one or more participle phrases. Be sure that you keep one main verb in the sentence; if you make all the verbs into participles, you will end up with a sentence fragment. In a few cases, we have starred the sentence that might best serve as the base sentence.

Example

The children peered into the darkness.
The children listened for the loud scratching to come again.

Listening for the loud scratching to come again, the children peered into the darkness.

or

Peering into the darkness, the children listened for the loud scratching to come again.

or

The children, listening for the loud scratching to come again, peered into the darkness.

or

The children peered into the darkness, listening for the loud scratching to come again.

1. Shawn Kemp batted the ball toward the basket.
   Shawn Kemp hung suspended in air.
2. Steve Young looked down the field.
   He found the place that Jerry Rice would reach in time to catch the ball.
3. The dirt bikes climbed the mountain trail.
   The dirt bikes trailed dust.
   The dirt bikes roared in the desert air.
4. The clouds streaked across the sky.
   The clouds were bringing rain.
5. The espresso was made from an instant mix.
   The espresso was extremely sweet.
6. Near the old farmhouse, the tractor sat abandoned.
   The tractor was collecting dust.
   The tractor was collecting spiders.
   The tractor was collecting bird nests.
7. After the picnic, Chen relaxed in the shade of the trees.
   Chen listened vaguely to the conversations around him.
8. The trees on the Monterey Peninsula are battered by ocean winds.
   The trees on the Monterey Peninsula are shaped by the ocean winds.
   The trees on the Monterey Peninsula stand as sentinels on the western edge of the continent.
9. Gail swam in the cool lake.
   Gail felt fish.
   The fish were bumping against her legs.
   *Gail made her way toward the island.
10. The cows stood in the meadow.
    The cows munched grass.
    The cows mooed occasionally.
11. The children were ordered to their seats.
    The children reluctantly stopped watching the commotion in the hall.
12. The combines moved across the grain-covered hills.
    *The combines cut the wheat in broad swaths.
    The combines were like giant insects.
13. Salmon swim upstream against the water flow.
    Salmon leap fifteen-foot waterfalls.

14. The dams were built to supply water to irrigate desert land.
    The dams were built to supply hydroelectric power.
    *The dams stop the salmon.
15. After the sunny weather, the seeds begin to sprout.
    The seeds poke the dirt up in miniature mountain ridges.
16. The hiker neared the top of the mountain.
    The hiker stepped dangerously near the edge.
17. The edge was carved by thousands of years of wind and snow and rain.
    *The edge scooped back.
    The edge then dropped a thousand feet to the valley floor.
18. The hiker looked at the view.
    The view was breathtaking.
    The hiker fell to her knees.
19. The wind whistled around her ears.
    The wind drowned out the sound of her own heartbeat.
20. The hiker returned to her car.
    The hiker was aware that she had had an experience.
    The experience was transforming.

B. Catching the Dangling Modifier

The following sentences contain dangling modifiers. Rewrite the sentences so that the problem is fixed. You might need to invent a subject or use a dependent clause in order to fix the problem.

Example

Peering into the darkness of the cave, a loud scream came from within.

Peering into the darkness of the cave, I heard a loud scream from within.

1. Wanting only peace and quiet, the bus roared down the street.
2. Standing on the corner, shifting from foot to foot, the light finally changed.
3. Not having eaten since breakfast, dinner arrived just before we began eating the salt in the salt shaker.

4. Grounded for two months by her father, anger filled her.
5. Searching through the wreckage left by the earthquake, a four-year-old boy was found by the rescuers.

C. Writing Your Own Participle Phrases

1. Write five sentences that use a participle phrase at the end of the sentence. (Example: *The gardener walked through her garden, grumbling about her weeds.*)
2. Write five sentences that use a participle phrase at the beginning of the sentence. (Example: *Crumbling his shredded wheat, the child waited for the milk.*)
3. Write five sentences that use a participle phrase between the subject and the verb. (Example: *The old picture album, buried beneath piles of yellowed letters, revealed some family secrets long kept in the closet.*)

D. Participle Phrases in Published Writing

Here is a passage by writer Diane Ackerman. Locate the participle phrases in the passage and comment on their use. How might the same information be conveyed without participle phrases? Compare the effects of other possible phrasings with the effect of the original.

> A hawk appeared, swooped, grabbed a bat straight out of the sky, and disappeared with it. In a moment, the hawk returned, but hearing his wings coming, the bats all shifted sideways to confuse him, and he missed. As wave upon wave of bats poured out of the cave, their collective wings began to sound like drizzle on autumn leaves. Gushing out and swirling fast in this living Mixmaster, newly risen bats started in close and then veered out almost to the rim of the bowl, climbing until they were high enough to clear the ridge. Already, a long black column of bats looked like a tornado spinning out far across the Texas sky. A second column formed, undulating and dancing through the air like a Chinese dragon, stretching for miles, headed for some unknown feeding ground. The night was silent except for the serene beating of their wings.
>
> Diane Ackerman, *The Moon by Whale Light and Other Adventures among Bats, Penguins, Crocodilians, and Whales* (New York: Random House, 1991), 6.

E. Combining in Context

In the following paragraphs, keep the focus and make the writing more effective by using participle phrases at one or more places in the paragraph.

1. Lewis and Clark readied themselves for the trip down the Snake and the Columbia. They made arrangements to leave their horses with the Nez Perce, hired two guides, and made dugout canoes. On October 16, 1805, they entered the Columbia. They passed a burial area on an island. They decided to stop. After they looked briefly at the human bones and wrapped bodies on the burial platform and at the horse bones around the platform, they pushed on. Along the river there were numerous Native American lodges and Native Americans. The Native Americans were splitting and drying the abundant salmon. Lewis and Clark traded trinkets for salmon, roots, and dogs, the latter being the favorite food of the expedition. They neared the big falls of the Columbia. They found the water getting more and more turbulent. At what is today called The Dalles, they had to portage all their food and equipment and lower the boats with lines along the southern edge. One boat got away when the line broke. This caused much excitement among the Indians who were watching and helping the expedition. Once they were below the falls, they found bigger, flatter, and highly decorated ocean-going canoes. They were near their goal, the mouth of the Columbia.
2. One night at Yosemite John Muir watched the moon on a waterfall. At midnight the moonlight made a rainbow 500 feet below where Muir stood. Muir decided to get behind the waterfall and watch the moonlight. The moonlight came through the water. He stepped out onto the rocky edge. He made his way along a ridge that was only six inches wide in one place. Suddenly the wind shifted. It sent water pounding down on Muir's head and shoulders. Muir knelt down. He waited for a chance to move farther back under the falls. He found a rock and a chunk of ice to wedge himself in. Finally the wind shifted again. Muir dashed for freedom. He escaped the ledge and made a fire to warm his numb limbs.

F. Revising Your Writing for Style

Choose a piece of your own writing and revise it by using participle phrases. Consider the following questions as you think about revising.

1. Are there places where the writing is repetitious and could be tightened with participle phrases?
2. Are there places where you could make the writing more effective, true, and clear by adding participle phrases?
3. Are there places where you could reinforce the meaning of the sentences by using participle phrases?

CHAPTER 11

INFINITIVE PHRASES

WHAT INFINITIVE PHRASES LOOK LIKE

1. **To enjoy life** is the hedonist's first goal.
2. It is difficult **to enjoy oneself endlessly.**
3. The American women hoped **to win their soccer games.**
4. Their goal was **to make women's soccer popular in the United States.**
5. The only way **to do that** is **to win games.**
6. Janine's writing process, **to rewrite and rewrite again,** proved successful.
7. Loretta irons **to avoid writing.**
8. The grammar teacher helped **Loretta change her attitude toward writing.**

How Grammarians Describe Infinitive Phrases

At their simplest, infinitives can be recognized as a verb form with no *-s, -ed,* or *-ing* ending and with a *to* in front of it. When there is a verb, not a noun, following it, the *to* does not introduce a prepositional phrase. As you can see from the preceding examples, infinitive phrases can perform a number of functions. They can function as nouns: in sentences 1 and 2 they are subjects, in sentences 3 and 8 direct objects, in sentences 4 and 5 subject complements, and in sentence 6 an appositive. They can also function as adjectives as in sentence 5 where *to do that* modifies *way.* And finally, they often function as adverbs, as in sentence 7, to mean *because* or *in order to;* in fact, the adverbial infinitive is often introduced with *in order to.*

Infinitives sometimes get more complicated than the gerunds and participles that we discuss in chapters 9 and 10. Here is an example:

Gingrich asked **the Republicans to vote for the Contract for America.**
Gingrich asked **them to vote for the Contract for America.**

Here the infinitive *to vote* has a subject, *Republicans* and *them;* notice that when the pronoun is used, it is in the object case, *them,* not the subject case, *they.*

In addition, there is an infinitive that does not use the *to* marker; this is called a simple infinitive. One use of the simple infinitive occurs when the infinitive is the object of certain prepositions, the most common being *but* (meaning "except"), *except,* and *besides.*

During the 1994 season, the baseball owners did nothing but **complain.**
During the 1994 season, the baseball players did nothing except **complain.**

Another use of the simple infinitive occurs when the infinitive is the direct object of *let, help, make,* and certain verbs of the senses such as *see, watch, hear,* and *feel.* This pattern is further complicated by the unmarked infinitive's also having a subject.

Jaime helped **his mother make latkes.**
Jaime helped **her make latkes.**

I saw **the cowboy capture her heart.**
I saw **him capture her heart.**

Notice that unlike the subject and verb in dependent and independent clauses, the pronoun subject is in the object case (*her* and *him*) and the verb does not take an *-s* to agree with the singular subject or an *-ed* to indicate tense.

Sometimes *for* is used as an expletive to introduce an infinitive phrase; usually when this introductory expletive is used, the infinitive phrase works as the subject of the sentence.

> For **Joe Montana to leave the San Francisco 49ers** was unthinkable.

Another variation on the infinitive phrase is to use it absolutely, as a kind of comment on the entire sentence.

> **To tell the truth,** I want to lie on the beach all summer.

Grammatically, infinitives complete verbs such as *hope, expect, want,* and *desire* that need an infinitive when the object indicates an action.

> He hopes **to join his wife on a vacation in France.**

Split Infinitives

You may have heard of split infinitives and the admonition never to use them. A **split infinitive** is an infinitive with an adverb between the *to* and the base verb.

> Marie vowed **to** *never* **ride a motorcycle again.**

The idea that they should never be split is based on seeing the *to* and the base verb as a single word that should never be separated. Today this rule is generally seen as a bit stuffy and as derived from Latin grammar, not based on English use.

How Infinitive Phrases Are Punctuated

Mostly, infinitive phrases are not punctuated. There are two exceptions. The first is an adverb infinitive at the beginning of a sentence—but not at the end.

> **To avoid her screaming children,** the mother slipped into the pool.
> The mother slipped into the pool **to avoid her screaming children.**

The second is an infinitive phrase that is a nonrestrictive appositive; it is set off with commas.

> By the end of the year, Ann hoped to reach her goal, **to be the first woman at the North Pole.**

What You Can Do with Infinitive Phrases

1. Choose an Infinitive instead of a Gerund as an Object

Some verbs can take either an infinitive or a gerund object when an action is the object, but there is usually a slight difference in meaning.

> They began **to expect the worst.**
> They began expecting the worst.

With the infinitive phrase in the first sentence, *to expect the worst* seems to be a onetime thing; with the gerund phrase in the second sentence, eternal pessimism seems to have set in.

2. Add Focus to Your Writing

The infinitive phrase used both as a direct object and as a subject can tighten the syntax and focus of the sentence. In the next example the revision using an infinitive phrase both shortens and sharpens a wordy original.

> Original: He hoped that he would be able to join his wife on a vacation in France.
> Revision: He hoped **to join his wife on a vacation in France.**

Only if there were a good reason to focus on *would be able* would you use the wordy noun clause rather than the infinitive phrase.

3. Control the Formality of Your Writing

Sometimes you can choose between a gerund and an infinitive as the subject of the sentence. Usually, the gerund phrase has a less formal feel, the infinitive phrase a more formal feel.

> Losing weight is the obsession of most American women.
> **To lose weight** is the obsession of most American women.

The formal sense of the infinitive as subject can be lost by using the delayed subject with the *it* expletive.

> *It* is the obsession of most American women **to lose weight.**

The delayed subject is more successful in some contexts than in others. This sentence may strike us as being less than clear and therefore less than effective. The following sentence, however, is quite clear and effective.

> *It* is necessary **to read the fine print.**

4. Create Effective Appositives for Other Infinitives

Infinitives can also make effective appositives for other infinitives. Notice that in the next sentence, the appositive works to give a definition of *rappel* in case your reader does not know what the word means, but in the second sentence, the appositive actually expands on the situation and gives another perspective on the lack of hope.

> In descending the cliff, they were forced **to rappel, to lower themselves by a rope passed under one thigh and over the opposite shoulder.**
>
> There was no reason **to hope for his return, to believe that he might have survived through the freezing night.**

5. Control Focus with Word Order

An adverbial infinitive phrase can come at the beginning or the end of the sentence, or between the subject and the verb.

> **To win their father's approval,** most men would do almost anything.
> Most men would do almost anything **to win their father's approval.**
> Most men, **to win their father's approval,** would do almost anything.

Notice the difference in emphasis that we get in the three versions. When the infinitive phrase comes first, it is emphasized. You are using the syntax to make part of the sentence boldface instead of highlighting text and clicking on boldface in your word processor. And it is far more effective than using boldface or an exclamation mark. The second of the preceding sentences is probably the most natural word order; you can use it when you have a matter-of-fact statement to make. And finally, in the third sentence you create some suspense; the reader must pay attention in order to solve the mystery and keep the meaning clear. Therefore, the whole sentence gets more emphasis than it normally would. You would use this order when you really want the reader to slow down and pay attention.

Other modifying structures in the sentence can also call for variation in word order.

> **To avoid starting his essay over,** Kendall began using the move, cut, and paste functions of his word processor.

It is also possible to put the infinitive phrase at the end of the sentence (as in the next example), but it is likely to get a little lost after the compound direct object and the prepositional phrase. In fact, the phrase might for a moment seem to be modifying *word processor.* Avoid this to keep from confusing your reader.

> ∅Kendall began using the move, cut, and paste functions of his word processor **to avoid starting over.**

Here is an example of a modification structure that requires the infinitive phrase to be at the end of the sentence.

> Lost in the woods, the little girl built a fire **to warm her hands.**
> ∅Lost in the woods, **to warm her hands,** the little girl built a fire.
> ∅**To warm her hands,** lost in the woods, the little girl built a fire.

6. Tighten the Syntax and Focus of Your Writing

An adverb clause can often be replaced by an infinitive phrase.

> Because she wanted to see Vince Gill smile at the girls, she bought a front-row ticket.
> **To see Vince Gill smile at the girls,** she bought a front-row ticket.
> She bought a front-row ticket **to see Vince Gill smile at the girls.**

The infinitive phrase is like a compressed adverb clause here. It is also true that there is some loss of focus on *wanted* in the reduction. The point is that you have choices; you need to choose the alternative that produces the meaning and effect that you want.

7. Create Coordination and Parallelism

In all its uses, the infinitive phrase can be effective in a series. If, for instance, you have several purposes for one action, using a series of infinitive phrases can be very emphatic.

Figure 11.1

Punctuating Infinitive Phrases

An infinitive phrase acting as an adverb at the beginning of the sentence is set off by a comma.

> **To learn effective and nonviolent methods of crowd control,** the police trained for months.

An infinitive phrase acting as a nonrestrictive appositive is set off by a comma.

> Tomorrow, Wei would begin to work at Microsoft, **to live the life she had always dreamed of.**

No other infinitive phrases are punctuated.

> MacNamara wrote his book **to explain his position, to clarify the record,** and **to make sure that the mistakes would not be made again.**

This is much clearer than using one infinitive and then shifting to some other structure.

> ∅MacNamara wrote his book **to clarify his position.** It was also important that he set the record straight, and he really wanted **to be sure that the same mistakes were not made again.**

This version does use infinitives, but in three totally different kinds of structures; the sentences wander, and before long the reader will wander away.

Often when infinitives are used in a series, the *to* is used only for the first item in the series and not for those that follow; that gives a slightly different effect from repeating the *to*.

> The plan was **to capture the village, take everything of value,** and **then burn the village to the ground.**

And finally, infinitive phrases used as both a subject and subject complement can provide a sentence balanced over the linking verb like the perfectly balanced scales of justice.

> **To marry Don Juan** is **to ask for a life of misery.**

EXERCISES

A. Practicing Sentence Combining

Combine each of the following pairs into one sentence that uses one or more infinitive phrases. Be sure that you have at least one independent clause for each sentence. The word ***this*** (in boldface) should be replaced with an infinitive phrase.

Example

Maureen rowed across the lake.
She wanted to see the marshland full of water lilies.
The lilies were pink and white.

Maureen rowed across the lake to see the marshland full of pink and white water lilies.

or

To see the marshland full of pink and white water lilies, Maureen rowed across the lake.

1. She wanted to find cheap fencing.
   She went to the suburbs.
2. Gerrard hoped for **this.**
   His hope was to find a cure for prostate cancer.
3. Andre expected to win the Boston Marathon.
   He also expected to become an Olympic medal winner.
4. There was tension and anxiety.
   This was when John was involved.
5. In the nineteenth century, doctors made a decision.
   The decision was that women's wombs would be removed.
   They did this surgery with the objective of curing women's hysteria.
6. The bride had done innumerable hours of physical therapy.
   She had done this so that she could walk down the aisle at her wedding.
7. **This** requires no special talent.
   The growing of orchids in one's house requires no special talent.
8. **This** is to be in touch with our deepest truths.
   We work with our dreams.

9. Alex climbed Mt. Rainier.
   She wanted to celebrate her fortieth birthday.
10. Ruby hung her clothes on the clothesline.
    She wanted the wind to fluff them
    She wanted the sun to dry them.
11. Frank Chin expected **this.**
    Jeffery Paul Chan expected **this.**
    The expectation was to create an anthology of Asian American writing.
12. They contacted Lawson Inada and Shawn Wong.
    The contacting was for the purpose of finding help with their project.
13. The four of them did extensive research.
    They did this research so that they could find the earliest examples of Chinese and Japanese American writing.
14. They even found a way.
    The way was including writing from the detention cells on Angel Island in San Francisco Bay.
15. They traveled to California.
    The traveling was for the purpose of talking with John Okada's widow.
16. They chose the name *Aiiieeeee* for their anthology.
    They chose the name for a reason.
    The reason was to scorn the only word that American comics had allowed Asian Americans to say.
17. There was no reason.
    The reason was to believe that *Aiiieeeee* would be a success.
    The reason was to believe that Americans were ready to read the works of Asian Americans.
18. Because *Aiiieeeee* was successful, they decided something.
    The decision was to do another anthology.
    This anthology would be called *The Big Aiiieeeee.*
19. Since the publication of *The Big Aiiieeeee,* there is a need.
    The need is for a place where new Asian American writers can be published.
20. Now Vietnamese, Koreans, and Cambodians have a desire.
    That desire is to be heard as Americans.

B. Writing Your Own Infinitive Phrases

1. Write two sentences that use an infinitive phrase as a noun. (Example: *He hoped to win the lottery.*)
2. Write two sentences that use an infinitive phrase as an adjective. (Example: *Kleenex to wipe away tears was always on the counselor's desk.*)
3. Write two sentences that use an infinitive phrase as an adverb. (Example: *Lincoln was determined to save the Union.*)
4. Write three sentences that use coordination and/or parallelism with infinitive phrases. (Example: *I am telling you these things not to hurt you but to show that I care about you.*)
5. Write three sentences that have an infinitive subject and an infinitive subject complement. (Example: *To know her is to love her.*)

C. Infinitive Phrases in Published Writing

Here is a passage by writer Harold Kushner. Locate the infinitive phrases in the passage and comment on their use. How might the same information be conveyed without infinitive phrases? Compare the effects of other possible phrasings with the effect of the original.

> My dinner companion was telling me that the way to get through a life of tragedy and uncertainty was to accept it and yield to it, rather than fight it, like an Oriental wrestler using his opponent's weight and strength against him rather than trying to meet him head-on. But he also tried to tell me that the way to keep from going through life in constant pain was to lower your expectations. Do not expect life to be fair, and you will not have your heart broken by injustice. There have always been crime, corruption, and accidents, and there always will be. It is part of the human condition. (A teacher of mine used to say, "Expecting the world to treat you fairly because you are a good person is like expecting the bull not to charge because you are a vegetarian.")
>
> Harold Kushner, *When All You've Ever Wanted Isn't Enough* (New York: Pocket Books, 1986), 91.

D. Combining in Context

In the following paragraphs, keep the focus and make the paragraph more effective by using infinitive phrases in one or more places in the paragraph.

Discuss the different versions that you and your classmates create. What are the strengths and weaknesses of each?

1. Builders are finding that there are ways in which they can economically use recycled items when they build. Recycled items have been available for several years, but in the past, the decision to use them meant that the builder would spend extra money. Now they can actually build more cheaply if they use some recycled and reclaimed items rather than if they use new items. Topsoil, concrete, and steel are being reclaimed and re-used rather than being sent to a landfill. Old paint turned in to household hazardous waste sites is mixed and recolored and used in public buildings. Concrete floor tiles are made from ground Mexican glass beer bottles. Even old carpet is being recycled. It is actually cheaper when they clean the carpet thoroughly; next they retexturize it; next they add designs and colors. This is cheaper than putting the old carpet in a landfill and buying new carpet. A public building in Seattle, the city known for its rainy weather, is practicing an ongoing form of recycling. It is collecting rainwater; the rainwater will be used for flushing toilets.
2. When people who speak different languages meet frequently so that they can trade, they need some way of communicating with one another. The same need arises in the colonization of another country or in workplaces where the workers (including slaves) may speak different languages from one another and from the boss. The language that is created in such situations is called a pidgin. Pidgins are made up of words from the languages of the contributing groups, but one language often contributes more than the others. So that it is pronounceable by all speakers, a pidgin cannot have sounds in it that are not present in all the contributing languages. In addition to this limitation in sounds, there is a very limited vocabulary, a vocabulary of nouns, verb, and adjectives. The words also usually have specific referents in the tangible world. Pidgin is a language that is used in order that a job gets done. Pidgins also lack clear syntax, with different people and even the same people arranging words differently when they mean the same thing. There are almost no purely structural words such as conjunctions and prepositions. Some pidgins remain pidgins forever or die out when the need for them disappears. Russonorsk is an example of such a pidgin. It was spoken in the nineteenth century by adult Russian and Norwegian fishermen so that they could transact business when they met together for brief visits in the Arctic. The speakers of this pidgin continued to speak their native languages when they communicated at

home and in their home country. But sometimes a pidgin gets spoken at home, and it takes the place of a native language for couples who do not speak one another's language. The children in this home need a language that expresses feelings and complex ideas; they need more words than those with tangible referents. And so within a couple of generations a creole is born. It seems that there is a natural language-making part of the brain that creates language when none is available. People need languages so that people can express the complexities of human experience, and the language-making part of the brain is there so that there is help to fulfill that need. Eventually creoles evolve into full-fledged languages with even larger vocabularies and complex grammars if the need is there.

E. Revising Your Writing for Style

Choose a piece of your own writing and revise it using infinitives. Consider the following questions when you think about revising.

1. Are there places where the writing could be tightened with infinitive phrases?
2. Are there places where you could make the writing more active by using an infinitive direct object?
3. Are there places where you could move the adverb infinitive phrase to make your writing more clear or forceful?
4. Are there places where you could use a series of infinitives or balance infinitive subjects and subject complements to create focus and coherence in your writing?
5. Do you want to change the formality of your writing by adding or subtracting infinitive phrases?

CHAPTER 12

NOMINATIVE ABSOLUTES

WHAT NOMINATIVE ABSOLUTES LOOK LIKE

1. The boats headed into the wind, **their sails trimmed.**
2. The tree stood on the hill, **its branches twisting in the wind.**
3. **Their tempers short, their anger ready to explode,** minorities are finally being listened to.
4. He looked at his wife, **his eyes twinkling.**
5. The wolf spider, **its fangs extended,** waits for its prey.
6. **The lightning having struck once,** we felt safe for the rest of the storm.
7. **His head cocked to one side, his tail pointing,** the spaniel stood in the middle of the yard, ready to chase the Frisbee.
8. **The river being polluted,** we had to carry our own drinking water.

How Grammarians Describe Nominative Absolutes

When we say that a structure is an **absolute** or used absolutely, we mean that the structure seems to relate not to just one word in the sentence, but to the entire sentence. The **nominative absolute** comes very close not just to relating to a sentence, but to being a sentence. It has what looks like a subject (*nominative* is just another word for subject form). In most cases, the nominative absolute is lacking only a form of the verb *be* (*am, is, are, was, were*) to be a complete sentence. In every sentence at the beginning of the chapter, except sentence 6, the nominative absolute can be made into a full sentence with an addition of a form of *be*.

> Their sails **were** trimmed.
> Its branches **were** twisting in the wind.
> Their tempers **are** short. Their anger **is** ready to explode.
> His eyes **were** twinkling.
> Its fangs **were** extended.

In sentence 6 (which has *having* plus a base verb), we need to substitute a present or past form of *have* rather than a form of *be* to make a full sentence from the nominative absolute.

> The lightning **had** struck once.

How Nominative Absolutes Are Punctuated

The punctuation of nominative absolutes is absolutely easy. They are always set off with a comma or commas.

> The militia made their charges, **their paranoia clear to all but themselves.**
> **His black eye-mask hiding his identity,** the Lone Ranger rode away.
> Grandfather Raven, **his magical skills intact,** slipped away.

The only variation on this punctuation is to use dashes instead of commas. The dash usually gives a less formal feel to the sentence, and it can also give added emphasis to the nominative absolute.

> The box—**its contents a mystery**—sat on the table.

What You Can Do with Nominative Absolutes

1. Add Detail

When a nominative absolute is used to add detail to a sentence, the base sentence gives a big picture and the nominative absolute is like a zoom lens, focusing on the details of the bigger picture.

> They looked at one another, **their hearts beating wildly.**
> **Their petals brilliant in the noonday sun,** the tulips colored the spring garden.

When the nominative absolute adds detail, it can come at the beginning of the sentence, at the end, or between the subject and the verb. The positioning of the absolute depends on various things—the meaning, the focus, the rhythm, the variety, and the context of the paragraph. You might discuss the differences in meaning, focus, and rhythm in the following.

> **His hat pulled low over his eyes,** the cowboy entered the saloon.
> The cowboy entered the saloon, **his hat pulled low over his eyes.**
> The cowboy, **his hat pulled low over his eyes,** entered the saloon.

2. Provide a Cause or Condition

The nominative absolute can express a condition or cause that has allowed the situation expressed in the base sentence to happen. Because causes come before effects, the material in the nominative absolute also implies a prior time in relationship to the base sentence.

> **Their rations running low,** the soldiers retreated to Lapwai.
> **Their muscles massaged,** the Jets took to the practice field.

If the information in the nominative absolute indicates a prior action but the absolute is positioned after the base sentence, the absolute may seem to be focusing on added detail rather than on the cause or prior condition.

> The Jets took to the practice field, **their muscles massaged.**

3. Vary the Focus

You may have been asking if *their* is really necessary in the previous sentences. The answer is that it is not. Sometimes the use or omission of the article (*a/an, the*) or possessive pronoun (*my, your, his, her, its, our, their*) is a matter of individual style; sometimes, however, the effect can also be different. Both articles and possessive pronouns are unstressed words in English, so if they are used to introduce a nominative absolute, they ease us into the structure on an unstressed syllable. When they are omitted, the effect is quite different; the nominative absolute begins with a bang on the stressed syllable of the subject of the absolute.

> The wolf spider waits for its prey, **its fangs extended.**
> The wolf spider waits for its prey, **fangs extended.**
> **Fangs extended,** the wolf spider waits for its prey.

Another variation on the nominative absolute, especially when it begins a sentence, is to place the preposition *with* before it. *With* in this case is an expletive, a word that has lost its usual meaning and functions only to signal a following pattern.

> **With its fangs extended,** the wolf spider waits for its prey.

4. Add Sophistication to Your Writing

The nominative absolute is a structure not frequently heard in spoken English; you almost never hear it in a conversation between two friends. It occurs in more public communication such as the TV news and weather reports, political speeches, and public addresses. But in spite of this scarcity in oral English, the structure is very much a part of written English, not so much in the newspaper as in essays and fiction. Ernest Hemingway used it extensively, thus saving his simple style from sounding simplistic.

> As they went up the hill in the dark, **the wind at their backs, the storm blowing past them as they climbed,** Anselmo did not feel lonely. [Ernest Hemingway, *For Whom the Bell Tolls* (New York: Charles Scribner's Sons, 1940), 200.]

According to one common classification of sentences, **simple sentences** contain one independent clause and no dependent clauses, and **complex sentences** contain at least one dependent clause. Dependent clauses certainly add one kind of complexity to a sentence, but nominative absolutes and verbal phrases add another. A simple sentence with a nominative absolute is anything but simple in the usual sense of the word. A nominative absolute is a sophisticated structure that can add detail and intensity to writing.

On the other hand, do not overdo it; you are not likely to find more than one or perhaps one series per paragraph in professional writing.

Figure 12.1
Punctuating Nominative Absolutes

Nominative absolutes are always set off by a comma or commas.

His mind having wandered during her question, he grunted a noncommittal answer.
The trees swayed in the wind, **their branches flailing like a person drowning.**
Its roof nothing but rotting struts, the old barn still stood erect, **its walls apparently impervious to rot.**

5. Create Coordination and Parallelism

The nominative absolute can be used quite effectively in a series of more than one nominative absolute or in a series that includes participle phrases. There can also be a nominative absolute in more than one place in the sentence or a nominative absolute in one place and participle phrases or appositive adjectives in another.

Lips painted red [nominative absolute], **eyelashes heavily mascaraed** [nominative absolute], Julia Roberts stood on the corner.
Head twisting from side to side [nominative absolute], **looking for prey** [participle phrase], the owl waited patiently.
Bulletproof vest securely fastened [nominative absolute], the officer walked down the hall, **the soles of his shoes clicking on the marble floor** [nominative absolute].
Its windows empty [nominative absolute], the unpainted house stood on the hill, **seeming deserted** [participle phrase].
Their lives nearly over [nominative absolute], the salmon struggle upstream, **exhausted** [participle].

Exercises

A. Practicing Sentence Combining

Combine each of the following pairs into one sentence that uses one or more nominative absolutes. Be sure that you have one base sentence, and remember that the information in the base sentence gives the bigger picture or the effect; the information in the nominative absolute is detail or cause. Discuss the different combinations that you and your classmates write. Consider, for instance, the effects of the five combinations in the example, and explain why we do not put the nominative absolute at the end of the sentence.

Example

Zorro made a Z in the air.
Zorro's sword was drawn.

His sword drawn, Zorro made a Z in the air.
or
Sword drawn, Zorro made a Z in the air.
or
With his sword drawn, Zorro made a Z in the air.
or
Zorro, his sword drawn, made a Z in the air.
or
Zorro, sword drawn, made a Z in the air.

1. In Andrew Wyeth's painting *Christina's World,* Christina kneels in the foreground.
   Her hands are grasping the dried grass.
2. The bus roared down the street.
   Its passengers grabbed for something to hang on to.
3. Their flags were at half-mast.
   The government offices were closed for an hour.
4. The lake shimmered in the moonlight.
   Its clear surface was cool and inviting.
5. The lights went out.
   The audience suddenly became silent.
6. Doan sat in the chair.
   His sprained ankle rested on the stool in front of him.
7. Katerina skated away.
   The blades of her skates reflected the colored lights of the arena.
8. Mark Spitz emerged from the water.
   His perfect dive was completed.
9. Their teeth are straightened.
   Their mouths are smiling.
   Middle-class children face the future with confidence.

10. Her body was emaciated.
    Her self-esteem was destroyed.
    The model entered the Betty Ford Clinic.

11. The Zuni *lhamanas* bridged the two genders.
    Their physiology was male.
    Their dress was female.
    Their cultural roles were both male and female.

12. Their clothes needed washing.
    The missionaries looked for a Zuni to do their laundry.

13. The roles of the *lhamana* were flexible.
    The *lhamana,* Wé Wha, was the only one in the pueblo who would do the laundry of outsiders.

14. The missionaries were outraged.
    Their religion found any deviation from two separate and distinct sexes sinful.

15. His hair was combed like a woman's.
    His dress was the clothing of a woman.
    Wé Wha was taken for a woman in Washington D.C.

16. The anthropologist Mrs. Stevenson had many male characteristics.
    Wé Wha seems to have considered her similar to himself.

17. The face of the *lhamana* was covered with the mask of the *Kolhamana* kachina.
    The *lhamana* played the role of the *lhamana* kachina in various ceremonies.

18. Today *berdache* is the word used by anthropologists to refer to Zuni *lhamanas* and to people fulfilling a similar role in other Native American tribes.
    Most Native American tribes in South, Central, and North America have a special place inside the community for third-gender people.

19. The knowledge of the history of the *berdache* in pre-Columbian America is being restored to gay Native Americans.
    Gay Native Americans have a new idea of their place in tribal life.

20. The gender designators of clothing and role in the community defined the *berdache* in Native American cultures.
    Therefore, *berdache* cannot be translated as "gay" or "homosexual."
    These terms refer only to sexual orientation in Western culture.

B. Writing Your Own Nominative Absolutes

Sometimes students have trouble making a distinction between a nominative absolute and a present participle phrase. Remember that if the nominative absolute includes a present participle, the nominative absolute has a subject in front of the present participle.

> *Nominative absolute:* their fingernails flashing
> *Participle phrase:* flashing their fingernails

1. Write five sentences that use nominative absolutes to add detail to a sentence. (Example: *The tourist entered the market, her purse clutched firmly in her hand.*)
2. Write five sentences that use nominative absolutes to add cause to a sentence. (Example: *Grandfather Raven, his gluttony knowing no bounds, asked for gifts of food.*)
3. Write five pairs of sentences (ten to fifteen sentences total) that vary the position of the nominative absolute and/or vary the use or non-use of the article or personal pronoun. (Examples: a. *His new bride mounted behind him, Tex rode out of town.* b. *Tex rode out of town, his new bride mounted behind him.*)
4. Write five sentences that use a series of nominative absolutes or a combination of nominative absolutes and participle phrases. (Example: *Eyes straight ahead, his body rigid, the Buckingham Palace sentry did not blink for the pretty tourist.*)
5. Write five sentences that use nominative absolutes at more than one place in the sentence. (Example: *The nomination already decided, the Republican Party trudges toward its convention, its sizzle gone.*)

C. Nominative Absolute Phrases in Published Writing

Here is a passage by writer Gregory Martin. Locate the nominative absolutes in the passage and comment on their use. How might the same information be conveyed without nominative absolutes? Compare the effects of other possible phrasings with the effect of the original.

> Then all them Boscos would show at the Overland in their funeral clothes and Aita would herd 'em into the recyvydor and the deceased would be laid out in a suit in a casket in the middle of the

room. (Aita kept the suit and the casket in the closet.) We might have fifty Boscos corralled in there. Ama would say a prayer and we'd all bow our heads and Aita would take a picture of everyone gathered around the open casket looking serious, the men with their hands behind their backs, the women fingering rosaries. And not long after, everybody'd go back to where they were before. Aita would send the photograph and a note to the family back in the old country.

Gregory Martin, *Mountain City*
(New York: North Point Press, 2000), 14.

D. Combining in Context

In the following paragraphs, keep the focus and make the paragraph more effective by using nominative absolutes in one or more places in the paragraph.

1. In the mid-October chill, the tomatoes still hang on the vines. Their peach and pale green tones aim toward ripeness. The nights are getting too cold, the days too short for me to hope that they will ripen here in the garden on the vine. If I leave them, they will succumb to slugs and split skins, and all manner of rot and decay. So I pick them, dozens of them, and bring them in to ripen. I try every method I know to bring them to ripe redness—brown paper bags, individual newspaper wrap, sitting in the open air on my counter. A few will make it. Their skin will be deep red, and their tomato smell and sweet acidy flavor will bring August into my late October kitchen.
2. Snow is late in Colorado this year. The skiers are sitting at home in shorts and T-shirts. Their skis are waxed. Their gear is packed. They are ready for fun. But La Niña keeps the weather warm and dry. Soon, however, the snows must come. A low pressure system from the west will meet a cold front from the north, and winter will arrive. The first big storm of the year will blanket the mountains in white, and the season will begin.

E. Revising Your Writing for Style

Choose a piece of your own writing and revise it using nominative absolutes. Consider the following questions when you think about revising.

1. Are there places that could use more detail? If so, would the nominative absolute effectively do that in the context?
2. Are there places where a nominative absolute would effectively indicate cause or prior condition?
3. Are there places where a nominative absolute might be an effective change of pattern or rhythm in the paragraph or paper?

13

CHAPTER

Coordination, Parallelism, and Balance

How Grammarians Describe Coordination, Parallelism, and Balance

Much of this chapter is a review of what we have already learned in chapter 5 and dealt with in almost every chapter. Because there is so much power in using coordination well, we are going to look at it one more time before we end.

When we have a series of two or more subjects, two or more verbs, two or more direct objects—two or more of any grammatical unit—we have coordination and parallelism; that is, there are two or more grammatical units that are coordinate—grammatically equal.

Coordination

Coordination involves a series of two or more, usually using conjunctions called coordinating conjunctions. We have already looked at the seven coordinating conjunctions that can be used between independent clauses: *and,* *but, or, nor, for, yet,* and *so.* Many of those coordinating conjunctions can also be used between subjects, verbs, direct objects, and other sentence elements when there are two or more of them.

> *Marcia* **and** *Louisa* baked a chocolate cake for their mother's birthday.
> They *frosted* the cake **and** *licked* the frosting knife.
> They ate *cake* **and** *ice cream* for dessert.
> They gave their *mother* **and** her new *husband* a surprise visit.

Of course *and* is not the only coordinating conjunction that can be used in these situations.

> *Jeanine* **or** *Wendy* will help you with your taxes.
> Lawrence was *honest* **but** *kind.*
> Reality is *harsh* **yet** *forgiving.*

There are also some coordinating conjunctions that work in pairs. We have already seen some subordinating conjunctions that work in pairs in chapter 8; coordinating conjunctions that work in pairs are called coordinating correlative conjunctions. Some common pairs are *both . . . and, either . . . or, neither . . . nor,* and *not (only) . . . but (also).* The basic rule for using coordinating correlative conjunctions is that whatever grammatical structure comes after the first conjunction in the pair must also come after the second conjunction in the pair. If there is an entire independent clause after the first conjunction in the pair, then there must be an entire independent clause after the second conjunction in the pair. Likewise, if there is a subject complement after the second conjunction in the pair, there must be a subject complement and only a subject complement after the first conjunction in the pair.

> **Both** *Karen* **and** her *sister* are getting married this summer.
> Alice is **neither** *at work* **nor** *at home.*
> Roscoe is **either** *tired* **or** *sick.*

We must be careful never to do the following.

> ∅**Either** Roscoe is tired **or** sick.
> ∅Alice **neither** is at home **nor** at work.

In the first sentence, a subject, verb, and subject complement come after *either,* but only a subject complement comes after *or.* In the second sentence, a verb and prepositional phrase come after *neither,* but only a prepositional phrase comes after *nor.*

The same rule is true for *not (only) . . . but (also);* however, there is an additional complication here. When *not only* comes before the subject and the verb, the word order is reversed from subject verb to verb subject in the first independent clause; in addition the verbs are limited to *be* or to a verb with an auxiliary. And in the second clause, the *but* is usually separated from the *also.*

Not only *is Marianne* a member of the board, **but** she is **also** the chair.
Not only *does Abraham* swim in the event, **but** he **also** dives.
Not only *will Jerome* arrive on time, **but** he will **also** arrive hungry.

When the *not only* comes before less than a whole clause, the order is not reversed.

Jamal **not only** swims **but also** dives.
Adrienne is **not only** intelligent **but also** kind.

Native speakers of English usually handle these complications without thinking, but English as a Second Language speakers have to think about them.

Parallelism

Parallelism is the use of coordinate elements as exemplified in all the preceding sentences. In other words, things that are coordinate are also parallel. The term **parallelism** to describe style is usually reserved for a series that involves more than two elements, and usually those elements themselves involve more than one word.

After the shouting, after the punching, after the knife throwing, Lawrence and Frieda would make up.
The president hoped **that the war would end, that the economy would improve,** and **that he would be reelected.**

It is very important when we write a series that all the elements in the series have the same syntactic function in the sentence. If the first two elements in the series are subject complements, then the third element must also be a subject complement, not a verb. An error in this is called faulty parallelism.

∅Stella is energetic, upbeat, and makes friends easily.
Stella is energetic, upbeat, and friendly.

∅Alexie is tall, muscular, and has big hands.
Alexie is tall and muscular and has big hands.

The second example cannot be corrected to *Alexie is tall, muscular, and big-handed* because *big-handed* is not a viable adjective. Instead we need to add a second verb to the sentence. Do not be afraid to use two *and*s near each other to connect different series.

Here is another problem sentence.

∅People of different cultures need to learn about one another's **needs, wants, skills,** and **benefit from each other.**

Needs, wants, and *skills* are all objects of the preposition *about;* so far, so good. But *benefit,* although it can be a noun, is an infinitive in this sentence; the sentence seems to be suggesting that people need two things, two infinitives: *to learn* and *to benefit.* The *to* does not have to be repeated with *benefit,* but it is there in the syntax of the sentence, and in this case, repeating it will help the reader interpret the sentence accurately.

People of different cultures need **to learn** about one another's needs, wants, and skills and **to benefit** from each other.

Notice that the *and* signals the end of one series; at that point another kind of series can be continued. In this case, the objects of the preposition end and the infinitives continue.

Balance

Balance is a term that is sometimes reserved for parallelism between sentences rather than within one sentence.

Before the Vietnam War, few Americans had heard of Vietnam. After the Vietnam War, few Americans have not heard of it.

As you can see, there is a repetition of structures here that is similar to parallelism. We could call this parallelism, but the repetition is not just of one structure—it is of every structure and of nearly every word. This gives a sense of balance, as though we have a teeter-totter perfectly balanced at the fulcrum. Balance is a powerful device for achieving coherence within a paragraph; just like road signs that warn of curves ahead, and the guardrails and white lines that mark the edges of strange roads for the driver, balance is a device that guides the reader through unknown territory.

This balance can also be achieved within a sentence.

> **To do your homework** is **to be ready for class.**
> **Laughing at one's parents** is **asking for trouble.**

It is not necessary that every part of the balanced structures be exactly the same, nor is it necessary in parallel structures that every part of the parallel elements be exactly the same. What is necessary is that the basic elements themselves be the same structure.

How Coordination, Parallelism, and Balance Are Punctuated

The widely accepted rule today for punctuating items in a series is to place a comma after each item, including the next-to-last one before the final conjunction, usually *and.* The rule bothers people who remember being taught to omit the comma before the final *and* or *or,* but it makes sense if punctuation is intended to help the reader follow sentences accurately. Sometimes we coordinate elements within a larger series of coordination; when we say such sentences aloud, we use pauses to indicate which elements belong together; in writing, the use and non-use of the comma does this.

> For breakfast, I like toast, bacon and eggs, **and** coffee.

A series of coordinate elements, especially longer ones, are sometimes interrupted by a word or phrase inserted for emphasis or explanation. This happens most frequently before the last item in a series. The interrupter is usually enclosed in a pair of commas or—for special emphasis—dashes.

> Kent is my roommate, my co-worker, and, **above all,** my friend.
> The disaster was blamed on the commanders in the field, on their superiors in Washington, and—**despite all the efforts of White House staffers**—on the president himself.

What You Can Do with Coordination, Parallelism, and Balance

1. Tighten, Clarify, and Strengthen Your Writing

Using coordination and parallelism can tighten and focus your sentences and paragraphs.

The newcomers were determined to take the land. One method they were prepared to try was persuasion. Force was also an option for them.

The newcomers were determined to take the land, either **by persuasion** or **by force.**

Notice the added power of taking the land *by force* in the second version, which is totally missing in the first version.

2. Focus on Comparison and Contrast

Parallelism lines things up so their similarities and differences stand out. This works in individual sentences as well as between paragraphs in a longer comparison and contrast discussion.

"We have always known that heedless self-interest was bad morals; we know now that it is bad economics." (Franklin D. Roosevelt, Second Inaugural Address, January 20, 1937.)

"Shallow understanding from people of good will is more frustrating than **absolute misunderstanding from people of ill will. Lukewarm acceptance** is much more bewildering than **outright rejection."** (Martin Luther King Jr., Letter from Birmingham Jail, April 12, 1963.)

Parallel elements can also use inverted order within a sentence to achieve a focus on the important element by placing it at the end of the sentence, creating suspense and a surprise ending.

He was kind and gentle **to his friends and co-workers; to his family,** he was a beast.

3. Combine Ellipsis and Repetition for Clarity and Effectiveness

The first sentence in the next example uses ellipsis to omit the bracketed words, words that are unnecessary because the parallelism makes the missing words clear to the reader. After that, the paragraph uses repetition with some variation to make a forceful point.

Communism's failures are seen as evidence of an unsound system, capitalism's [failures are seen] as exceptions to a sound one. When people go hungry in a communist country, we blame it on communism; when they go hungry in a capitalist society, we blame it on them. Communism has victims; capitalism, we assure ourselves, only has losers.

Sometimes we have been told to watch out for unnecessary repetition, and so we assume that all repetition is bad. Repetition is a problem when the idea is going nowhere. Repetition is not a problem when it is used to heighten the focus on the important words in a structure. When using parallelism for comparison or contrast in writing, vary only the words that count.

Training prepares you for a job; education gets you ready for life.
Training prepares you **for a job; education** prepares you **for life.**

Give me liberty or let me receive death.
"Give me **liberty** or give me **death.**" (Patrick Henry, March 23, 1775, speech advocating resistance to British policy.)

To be or not to exist, that is the question.
"To be or **not to be,** that is the question." (William Shakespeare, *Hamlet,* act 1, scene 1, line 55.)

I see one-third of a nation ill-clothed, not well housed, and insufficiently nourished.
"I see one-third of a nation **ill-housed, ill-clad, ill-nourished.**" (F. D. Roosevelt, Second Inaugural Address, January 20, 1937.)

4. Use Pairs and Triads

English speakers especially like parallelism in groups of two and three. One of us found the following in an anonymously written pamphlet in a doctor's office that describes ear-wax movement and middle-ear infection in groups of three. Surely it is a habit of mind and not a fact of nature that exactly three symptoms are listed for each medical problem; in fact, in one case two symptoms have been combined into one using coordination in order to make a total of three.

"Old ear wax is constantly being transported from the ear canal to the ear opening, where it usually **dries, flakes,** and **falls out.**"
"Infection in the middle ear **causes earache, a red inflamed eardrum,** and **a buildup of pus and mucus behind the eardrum.**"

Here are two more examples.

Jeff likes **swimming, skiing and snowboarding,** and **sailing.**
One current Republican proposal would remove taxes from **bank account interest, capital gains and other investment income,** and **all inheritances.**

FIGURE 13.1
Punctuating Coordination

Two items in a coordinate series are connected with a coordinating conjunction with no punctuation.

Christa and James picnicked at Deception Pass.
Maureen and Bob drove to **California and Nevada** on their vacation.

In a series of three or more coordinate items, all of the elements are generally separated with commas.

Casey has attended **Cedar Park Community College, University of Chicago, University of Illinois,** and **Ball State University.**

5. Omit the Final Coordinating Conjunction

It can sometimes be effective to omit the coordinating conjunction that signals the end of a coordinate series. Frequently the effect of doing this is to give the sense that this is only part of a list that could go on and on. It also tightens the writing, giving a sense of tension.

Maureen tried too hard **to spend time with her children, to cook interesting meals for her husband, to provide for her retirement, to do the housework, to feed her own creativity.**

EXERCISES

A. Practicing Sentence Combining

Combine or revise the following sentences using coordination, parallelism, and balance.

Example

Joan likes desserts.
Joan does not like sweet desserts.

Joan has a rich tooth.
She does not have a sweet tooth.

Joan likes desserts, but she does not like sweet desserts; she has a rich tooth, not a sweet tooth.

1. Benjamin got as far as he got by being several things.
   He was hardworking.
   Thriftiness was another of his qualities.
   He practiced honesty.
   This last quality was important above all the others.
2. Shakespeare's history plays show something about the qualities that make a good king.
   They may be different from the characteristics that go into the creation of a good person.
3. Our conversation last night went a long way toward resolving some of our differences.
   Also, communication between us was improved by it.
   In the end, it has made our whole future together look much brighter.
4. Patriotism consists not only of waving your country's flag.
   The attempt to correct your country's faults is also part of patriotism.
5. At the beginning of the year, they were inseparable lovers.
   This had changed completely twelve months later.
6. Couples were everywhere.
   They whirled around the dance floor in the ballroom.
   They were whispering in corners of the terrace.
   Into the deep shadows of gardens beyond some wandered.
7. He thought he was cheating the system.
   It was he himself who got cheated.
8. The digestive process begins in the mouth.
   The stomach is where the digestive process continues.
   The completion of the digestive process is in the intestines.
9. As Martin Luther King Jr. pointed out, freedom is not usually given to the oppressed.
   Usually the oppressed take it from the oppressor.
10. A home computer can do many things.
    It can keep track of your finances.
    It is capable of becoming a whole shopping center at your fingertips.

Turning on your coffeemaker at different times on different mornings is among its capabilities.
It can be programmed to read the weather report and decide whether to run the sprinkler system.
Your alarm system can be run by the computer.
How about having it remind you that your mother's birthday is coming up?
If you want to make up your own poem about how much she means to you, it can even supply you with rhyming words.

11. Some people consider multiculturalism a dangerous trend in the United States.
    In the opinion of others, it could be better described as an important goal.
    A third group views it as a simple fact of life in this country.
12. That we are now a nation of many cultures seems beyond question.
    That many religions exist in this nation seems beyond question.
    That ethnic identities come in many varieties in this nation seems beyond question.
13. Until recently, the nation thought of itself as a melting pot that people went into Italian or German or Russian Jewish.
    They came out with an American identity.
14. Because this American identity was essentially white European in origin, the melting pot worked somewhat well for European immigrant groups with white skin.
    Others experienced it less favorably.
15. People of non-European ethnicity or skin color were often excluded from the melting pot by various factors.
    Laws were one factor.
    They were also excluded by business practices.
    Another factor was social prejudice.
16. Even those who could assimilate did so at a price.
    The price included giving up their own cultural practices.
    They never saw their experiences and contributions reflected in the country's history books.
17. This has led some people to call for the replacement of the idea of a melting pot.
    They prefer the salad bowl image, in which ingredients retain their identities while making their distinctive contributions to the flavor of the whole.

18. Others do worry that it is not possible to have two things at once.
    One would be cultural diversity.
    The other would be a condition of being nationally unified.
19. Multiculturalists answer that it is not a matter of possibility.
    It is simply necessary.
20. It is also, in their view, a glorious opportunity to achieve a nation even richer that the one we already have.
    It would be stronger too.
    Also, it would be even more beautiful.

B. Writing Your Own Parallel and Balanced Sentences

1. Write three sentences that use a series of three or more prepositional phrases. (Example: *Gilgamesh journeys under a huge mountain, over a glittering sea, across the waters of death, and finally on to a forested island.*)
2. Write five sentences that use a series of subject complements. (Example: *He was tall, dark, handsome, and utterly boring.*)
3. Write three sentences that use effective repetition in a series or in balanced sentences or independent clauses. (Example: *Science can tell us how we got here; faith can tell us what we are here for.*)
4. Write three sentences that effectively eliminate *and* before the final word in a series. (Example: *They were brought closer together in their marriage by their common recognition that each of us is essentially single, separate, solitary.*)

C. Coordination, Parallelism, and Balance in Published Writing

Here is a passage by writer Jared Diamond. Locate the coordination and parallelism in the passage and comment on their use. How might the same information be conveyed without coordination and parallelism? Compare the effects of other possible phrasings with the effect of the original.

> We have seen that large or dense populations arise only under conditions of food production, or at least under exceptionally productive conditions for hunting-gathering. Some productive hunter-gatherer societies reached the organizational level of chiefdoms, but none reached the level of states; all states nourish their citizens by food production. These considerations, along with the just

mentioned correlation between regional population size and societal complexity, have led to a protracted chicken-or-egg debate about the causal relations between food production, population variable, and societal complexity. Is it intensive food production that is the cause, triggering population growth and somehow leading to a complex society? Or are large populations and complex societies instead the cause, somehow leading to intensification of food production?

Jared Diamond, *Guns, Germs, and Steel: The Fates of Human Societies* (New York: W. W. Norton, 1997), 284.

D. Combining in Context

In the following paragraphs, keep the focus and make the writing more effective by using parallelism and balance at one or more places in the paragraph. Consider this a kind of final exam. Use all that you know about the syntax that you have worked with in this book. There is no one right answer. Compare your paragraphs with your classmates'; what are the strengths and perhaps weaknesses of each version?

1. Although she was in love with at least two men during her life and her councilors and Parliament also pushed her to marry, Elizabeth I had many reasons to remain a virgin queen. She did not want to be ruled by a man. The rules of marriage at that time dictated that a married woman was ruled by her husband. Succession was another problem that she was concerned about. If she had a son, there would be many in England who would be drawn to a rebellion around her son, who would be a male ruler. There were also many in the rest of Europe who would like the same thing. It is also possible that Elizabeth was afraid that she might die in childbirth. It was certainly not uncommon for a young healthy woman to die in childbirth in late medieval times. Not marrying also made it possible for Elizabeth to fashion herself the Virgin Queen, a Protestant replacement for the Virgin Mary. Elizabeth had herself dethroned the Virgin Mary when as a Protestant she succeeded her Catholic half-sister. As the Virgin Queen, she could be married only to the people of England and thus claim their adoration and loyalty.
2. On Memorial Day, Mom will come. She will have Grandma and aunts and uncles with her. They will come with flowers in hand. They will also have hoes and even rakes in hand. They will come in a procession up the hill to your corner. While they walk, they will chatter about the

flowers on Uncle Dan's grave. They will also be talking about the weeds on Aunt Adeline's grave. And they will mention the new curb around Conrad's plot and the plastic flowers Bucks always bring. They will even talk about the Wolfrums, who never come at all. The weeds will be pulled from your plot by them, and they will pour water over your stone to wash off the dust of spring plowing. They will rake the sand into straight lines. Peonies, lilacs, and coral bells in a foil-covered can will be left by them over your bones as will a yellow rose on your tombstone. Do they hear the silence into which the meadowlark sings?

E. Revising Your Writing for Style

Choose a piece of your own writing and revise it by using coordination, parallelism, and balance. Consider the following questions as you think about revising.

1. Are there places where the writing is repetitious and could be tightened with coordination, parallelism, or balance?
2. Are there places where you could more effectively point to comparison and contrast elements by using coordination, parallelism, or balance?
3. Are there places where you could combine ellipsis and repetition for clarity and effectiveness?
4. Are there places where you could effectively use a longer series of three or even more? Would it work to omit the final coordinating conjunction or to use an interrupting modifier to add clarity or information?

Glossary of Grammatical Terms

active voice see **voice.**

adjectival a word or structure that functions as an adjective in a sentence, modifying a noun.

adjective a form-class word whose main function is to modify a noun or be a subject complement. Adjectives often have such endings as *-ous, -able, -ible,* and *-ish,* and they can take the *-er* and *-est* suffixes for purposes of comparison. Example: *My **collapsible** umbrella is **smaller** than yours.*

adverb a form-class word that modifies verbs. (Adverbs are traditionally described as modifying adjectives and other adverbs as well as verbs, but contemporary grammarians prefer to call such modifiers **qualifiers.**) Adverbs often end in *-ly,* and some can take *-er* and *-est* endings to express comparison. Example: *The announcer spoke **clearly*** but ***faster** than most.*

adverb clause a dependent clause whose principal sentence function is to modify verbs; it can also modify adjectives and adverbs. Adverb clauses are typically introduced by subordinating conjunctions such as *because, although, when, after,* and *if.* Example: *Neil was upset **because birds had eaten all the cherries.***

adverbial a word or structure that functions as an adverb. Common adverbials are prepositional phrases and adverb clauses.

appositive a noun or noun phrase that renames another other noun and fills the same grammatical slot in a sentence as the noun it renames. Example: *My mother, **a chef,** works on weekends.*

appositive adjective an adjective that is placed and punctuated in such a way that it receives a focus in a noun phrase different from that of regular adjectives. Appositive adjectives usually occur in pairs or threes. Whether preceding or following the noun, they are set off by punctuation (usually commas); when preceding a noun that has a determiner, they come before the determiner. Examples: *The apricots, **ripe and flavorful,** made wonderful jam. **Soft and sweet,** the pears were perfect for the baby.*

auxiliary verb a type of verb that helps indicate time (tense) and whether an action is in a state of completeness or is still in progress (aspect). Common auxiliary verbs include forms of *be, have, do, can, will, may,* and several others. Examples: *The tide **has** turned. The main branch of the library **will be** rebuilt.*

base sentence the independent clause of a sentence. Example: *After the human genome is mapped, **the real work begins.***

base verb the part of the verb that carries the dictionary meaning. Examples: *Roger **loves** to fish. Roger has **quit** fishing.*

clause a group of words that has a subject and a predicate. An **independent clause** can stand alone as a sentence. A **dependent clause** cannot stand alone as a sentence; it is usually introduced by a subordinator, a word that makes the clause dependent. A dependent clause must be attached to an independent clause. Example: *Water flooded the valley* [independent] *when the dam broke* [dependent].

complement a word or structure that completes a transitive or linking verb. Common complements include direct objects and subject complements. Examples: *Ford builds* ***automobiles.*** *Pie cherries are* ***sour.***

complete subject see **subject.**

complex sentence a sentence with one independent clause and one or more dependent clauses. Example: *Crocus emerge from the ground when the days lengthen in late January.*

compound sentence a sentence that contains more than one independent clause and no dependent clause. Example: *Modern physics has opened up new views of space and time, and modern biology has made equal strides in understanding the basis of life.*

compound-complex sentence a sentence that contains more than one independent clause and one or more dependent clauses. Example: *When the earthquake shook the city, old brick buildings that were built on landfill collapsed, and even newer earthquake-proof buildings had broken windows.*

conjunction a structure-class word that functions to join words and structures in a sentence.

conjunctive adverb a structure-class word, such as *however, therefore, moreover,* and *nevertheless,* that helps connect one independent clause to another while modifying the second clause. A conjunctive adverb usually comes at the beginning of the second clause and is preceded by a semicolon (not a comma) and followed by a comma. Example: *The bridge should be strengthened against earthquakes;* ***however,*** *the state has no funds for this purpose.*

coordination the joining of two or more grammatically equal units of a sentence. These may include anything from single words to full clauses. Examples: ***Jack*** *and* ***Jill*** *went up the hill. Albert believes* ***that we have overemphasized the intellectual*** *and* ***that we must focus more on the spiritual.*** See also **parallelism.**

coordinating conjunction a word that joins words or structures that have identical functions in a sentence. The coordinating conjunctions are *and, but, or, nor, for, yet,* and *so.* Examples: *Ralph* ***and*** *his brothers ride the school bus to school every day. I wish I could go to Hawaii with you,* ***but*** *I am busy the week you are going.*

coordinating correlative conjunctions a pair of coordinate conjunctions that function together to connect words or groups of words that are structurally equal, such as *not (only) . . . but (also), either . . . or, neither . . . nor,* and *both . . . and.* Example: ***Both*** *Nadine* ***and*** *her twin sister Nancy became teachers.*

dangling modifier a modifier that does not clearly modify a word in the sentence; sometimes there is not even a word for it to modify. All verbals can be dangling modifiers, but the dangling participle is the most common. Example: ∅***Nearing the scene of the accident,*** *silence overcame us.*

dependent clause see **clause.**

determiner a structure-class word that signals a noun and modifies it, usually by limiting it in some way. Common determiners include *the, a/an, this, these, my, our, some, any, one, two, first,* and *second.* Examples: ***The*** *man in* ***the*** *front row is* ***a*** *professional athlete.* ***My*** *second car is* ***a*** *truck.*

direct object the noun or noun substitute that receives the action of a transitive verb, usually answering the questions what? and whom? Examples: *The bald eagle snatched the young* ***heron*** *out of its nest. The scene shocked some* ***viewers.***

elliptical structure a structure in which some words necessary to the grammar of the sentence are omitted because they can be interpreted as understood. Examples: *When* [you are] *making pastry, keep the dough cold. Judy is as tall as Harold* [is tall].

expletive a word that carries no semantic meaning in a sentence but sits in the position where a word, phrase, or clause that does carry meaning would ordinarily sit. The displaced structure generally appears after the verb. Examples: ***There*** *are twenty-six letters in our alphabet.* ***It*** *is difficult to water ski barefooted.*

form the outward grammatical features of a word, such as its spelling and pronunciation. That nouns take a final *-s* when they are plural is an aspect of their form.

form classes the four parts of speech—noun, verb, adjective, adverb—that contain most of the content words in English. The classes are open to new words. The addition of *-s* to make nouns plural and *-ed* to indicate past tense in verbs are aspects of form. See also **structure classes.**

fragment a group of words punctuated as a sentence but missing a subject, verb, or both. Examples: *Near the falls. After the winter storm collapsed the barn.*

function what a word or structure can do in the syntax of a sentence and where it can be placed. That a noun can be the subject of a verb and that it can follow *the* are two aspects of its function.

gerund a verbal that ends in *-ing* and functions in sentences as a noun. Example: ***Jogging*** *raises your heart rate.*

gerund phrase a gerund plus its complements and modifiers. Example: *I love* ***visiting New York in the spring.***

helping verb see **auxiliary verb.**

independent clause see **clause.**

indirect object a noun or noun substitute that functions together with a direct object to complete certain transitive verbs. The indirect object is usually the receiver of the direct object. Example: *The college gave* ***Toni*** *a scholarship.*

infinitive a verbal usually marked by *to* followed by the uninflected verb (no *-s, -ed,* or *-ing* ending); infinitives function as nouns, adjectives, and adverbs. Sometimes the infinitive is not marked with *to,* and sometimes the infinitive can have a subject (this will be in the object form if it is a personal pronoun). The unmarked infinitive is called a **simple infinitive;** this is the form of the verb that you find in the dictionary. Examples: *Liliane wants* ***to leave*** *the committee. Charlie helps* ***his mother water*** *the flowers. Jerome asked* **God to give** *him a vision.*

infinitive phrase an infinitive plus its complements and modifiers. Example: *Marianne wanted* ***to leave the old plantation untouched.***

inflection an element of a word added to a root that changes the form of the word, often resulting in change in function. Common inflections are *-ing, -ed, -ly,* and *-s.* Examples: *runn**ing**, root**ed**, kind**ly**, snow**s**.* See also **suffix.**

intransitive verb a verb that requires no complement to be complete. Example: *The children* ***slept.***

irregular verb a verb that has past tense and past participle forms that do not end in *-ed;* many of our most commonly used verbs are irregular. Example: *The cat* ***comes*** *home every night. The dog* ***came*** *home last night. Both the dog and the cat* ***have come*** *home.*

linking verb a verb that requires a subject complement to be complete. The most common linking verb is *be* (*am, are, is, was, were*); others are *become, seem, look, feel,* and *taste.* Examples: *The Herlichs* ***are*** *my neighbors. Their garden* ***looks*** *beautiful.*

main verb see **base verb.**

modifier a word or structure that gives information about another word or structure in a sentence. Modifiers include adjectives and adverbs, nouns adding information to other nouns, and determiners and qualifiers. Examples: *The* ***young*** *tennis player played* ***very well.***

nominative absolute a syntactic structure that has a subject but not a complete verb, and that relates to the sentence as a whole rather than to one word or group of words in the sentence. Examples: ***Their lights flashing, their sirens screaming,*** *the fire trucks tore down our street after midnight last night.*

nonrestrictive clause/phrase an adjectival structure containing information necessary to distinguish the noun that it modifies from all similar things that noun might be referring to. Examples: *My petunias,* ***which I water regularly,*** *still look wilted. Walt Whitman's one book,* ***Leaves of Grass,*** *was revised and republished many times.*

noun a form-class word that can be made plural or possessive. Nouns typically name persons, places, things, and abstractions. Examples: *The* ***twins*** *showed many* ***similarities.***

noun clause a dependent clause that can perform the same sentence functions as noun phrases. They can be subjects, direct objects, subject complements, objects of the preposition, and appositives. Example: *I believe* ***that people from Earth will one day walk on Mars.***

noun phrase a noun plus its modifiers.

noun substitute a word or structure that can be placed where nouns are placed in a sentence. The most common noun substitutes are **pronouns;** others include

gerunds, infinitives, and **noun clauses.** Examples: ***She*** *loves* ***swimming,*** *but* ***he*** *prefers* ***to sit on the beach.***

object complement the word or structure that functions together with a direct object to complete certain transitive verbs, renaming or describing the direct object. It may be a noun or an adjective. Examples: *The company named Rodolfo* ***manager.*** *They consider him* ***capable.***

object of the preposition see **preposition.**

parallelism a series of three or more coordinate sentence units in which each unit contains more than one word and the words of each unit are coordinate with words in the other units. Example: *Conditions were so poor that doctors had to* ***treat infections without antibiotics, dress wounds without bandages,*** *and* ***perform surgery without anesthetics.*** See also **coordination.**

participial phrase see **participle phrase.**

participle a verbal that usually functions as an adjective. The **present participle** ends in *-ing* and indicates intransitive or transitive active **voice.** The **past participle** ends in *-ed* or takes the verb's irregular past participle form and indicates passive **voice.** Examples: *The* ***running*** *water seemed to bother no one. The* ***broken*** *cup cannot be mended. The* ***coming*** *events will not please everyone. The woman* ***speaking*** *just won an award. I don't like* ***burned*** *toast.*

participle phrase a participle plus its complements and modifiers (also sometimes called a participial phrase). Example: ***Nearing the old cemetery,*** *the teenagers sobered.*

passive voice see **voice.**

past participle see **participle.**

personal pronoun a structure-class word that substitutes for a specific noun; see chart in appendix D.

phrase a group of words lacking a subject-verb combination and functioning as a unit in a sentence. Examples: ***near the house, the forbidden pleasures.***

predicate a structure that includes the verb and the words associated with it; it is made up of a verb phrase, but it may also have a noun phrase in it. The predicate makes a statement about the subject. In phrase-structure grammar, predicate and **verb phrase** are the same thing: both include all auxiliaries, modifiers, and complements. Example: *Farouk* ***made a beautiful strawberry tart for dessert.***

preposition a structure-class word that precedes a noun or noun substitute, called the **object of the preposition.** Some prepositions are **with, through, in, up,** and **between.** Examples: *The cat is* ***in*** *the tree. I slept* ***during*** the concert.

prepositional phrase a group of words beginning with a preposition and ending with its object. A prepositional phrase shows a relationship between its object and the word that the phrase modifies. Prepositional phrases generally function as adjectives or adverbs, but they occasionally function as nouns. Examples: *The woman* ***on the white horse*** *is wearing her hair* ***over her naked shoulders. Between 12:00 and 2:00*** *is the best time to find me home* ***during the day.***

present participle see **participle.**

pronoun a word that substitutes for a noun or noun phrase and in many cases refers to a specific noun or noun phrase. Examples: *The tree stood stark and alone on the hilltop;* ***it*** *completely blocked the moon from* ***my*** *sight.* ***Everyone*** *is coming to the party at Jill's tonight.* See also **personal pronoun.**

qualifier a structure-class word that precedes an adjective or adverb and modifies it, usually by increasing or decreasing the quality it signifies. Examples: ***very*** *hot,* ***quite*** *cold,* ***rather*** *nice,* ***too*** *well.*

regular verb a verb with past tense and past participle forms ending in *-ed;* most verbs in English are regular, and all new verbs added to the language are regular.

relative adverb a word that functions as an adverb when introducing relative clauses. These include *when, where,* and *why.* Example: There was a time **when** you were happy to sit and do nothing.

relative clause a dependent clause beginning with a relative pronoun or a relative adverb. Example: *The ice cream* ***that I bought two hours ago*** *has melted!*

relative pronoun a word belonging to a class of pronouns that introduces relative clauses. Some relative pronouns are *who, whom, whose, which,* and *that.* Example: I was in a plane **that** felt as if it were running over the baggage cart when the earthquake hit.

restrictive clause/phrase an adjectival structure containing information necessary to distinguish the noun that it modifies from all similar things that noun might be referring to. Examples: *The man* ***who wrote this book*** *seems to hate women. Gerald's book* ***The Wisdom of Women*** *is not an easy read.* [Gerald has written more than one book.]

simple infinitive see **infinitive.**

split infinitive an infinitive with an adverb between the *to* and the verb. A split infinitive is often considered nonstandard English language use, but that perspective is changing. Example: *He promised* ***to*** *never* ***quit loving me.***

structure classes the parts of speech that help set up the structural relations among words, phrases, clauses, and sentences. The structure classes include pronouns, determiners, prepositions, and conjunctions. They are considered closed: new words are not added, as they are to the form classes. See also **form classes.**

subject the noun or noun substitute that names what the predicate of a sentence is about. The **complete subject** is made up of the subject plus its modifiers. Example: ***Whales*** *cavorted in the moonlight.* ***A school of humpback whales*** *cavorted in the moonlight.*

subject complement the word or structure that completes a linking verb. It may be a noun or an adjective. Examples: *Greg is a* ***poet.*** *He may become* ***famous.***

subordinating conjunction a word that introduces a dependent clause and connects the dependent clause to other structures in the sentence. Many grammarians today limit the definition to words that introduce adverb clauses. The list includes *when, where, if, although, while,* and *after.* Examples: *Marcel postponed his picnic until **after** it quit raining.*

subordinating correlative conjunctions a pair of subordinating conjunctions that function together, the first in the main clause and the second in the dependent clause. Common pairs include *so . . . that, as . . . as,* and *if. . . then.* Example: *Jody has gone **as** far **as** she can go.*

subordinator a word that introduces a dependent clause and makes it dependent. Common subordinators are **relative pronouns,** such as *who, that,* and *which;* and **subordinating conjunctions,** such as *when, if,* and *because.* Examples: *People **who** leave New York often return **because** they miss the city's energy and variety.* See also **clause.**

suffix an addition to the end of a word that alters its meaning or part of speech. Suffixes are commonly found at the end of nouns and adjectives. Examples: *intelligen**ce**, founda**tion**, contagi**ous**, child**ish**.* See also **inflection.**

tense a grammatical feature of verbs that relates to time. Verbs show tense by changing form. Example: *I **play** tennis almost every week; I play**ed** tennis last week.*

transitive verb a verb that requires at least one complement, a direct object, to be complete. Example: *Dimitri **makes** furniture.*

verb a form-class word that changes form to show past tense and functions with a subject to make a statement about the subject. Example: *The ambulance **collided** with the fire truck.* See also **intransitive verb; irregular verb; regular verb; transitive verb.**

verb phrase a verb, its auxiliaries, and its modifiers. Example: *The police car **has driven down this street many times this week.*** See also **predicate.**

verbal a word formed from a verb but functioning as something other than a verb in the sentence. See also **gerund; infinitive; participle.**

voice a quality belonging only to transitive verbs that shows the relation between the subject and verb, with the subject either doing or receiving the action. In an **active voice** sentence, the subject does the action of the verb and the direct object receives the action. In a **passive voice** sentence, the word that was the object in the active voice sentence becomes the subject; the subject of the active voice sentence may or may not appear in a prepositional phrase beginning with *by;* and, finally, the verb consists of a form of the auxiliary *be* and the past participle of the base verb. Examples: *Crystal **ate** the ice cream too fast.* [active voice] *The ice cream **was eaten** too fast.* [passive voice] *Elaine **courted** Daniel for months.* [active voice] *Daniel **was courted** (by Elaine) for months.* [passive voice]

APPENDIX A

Common Surface Problems

As we say in our introductory section "To the Student," this is a book about what you can do, not what you cannot do. We strongly believe that this is what student writers should concentrate on. Nevertheless, especially in formal writing, certain rules and conventions are widely observed, and when you break them, you risk drawing your reader's attention away from what you are saying to some surface detail of grammar, punctuation, or usage. Sometimes, you even risk confusing your meaning. Below is a selected list of common problems of this kind along with marginal symbols that editors and writing instructors use to mark them. Following the list is a brief explanation of each item with examples showing how to fix the problem.

,	1.	**Comma**
	1a.	Missing comma with an introductory element
	1b.	Missing comma in a compound sentence
	1c.	Missing comma in a series
	1d.	Missing comma(s) with nonrestrictive element
	1e.	Incorrect comma(s) with restrictive element
	1f.	Incorrect comma after *is, was,* or other forms of *be*

;	**2.**	**Semicolon**
	2a.	Missing semicolon before a conjunctive adverb in a compound sentence
	2b.	Incorrect semicolon setting off a phrase or dependent clause
'	**3.**	**Apostrophe**
	3a.	Missing or misplaced possessive apostrophe
	3b.	Its/it's confusion
agr	**4.**	**Agreement**
	4a.	Lack of subject-verb agreement
	4b.	Lack of pronoun-antecedent agreement
cs	**5.**	**Comma splice**
dm	**6.**	**Dangling modifier**
frag	**7.**	**Fragment**
fs	**8.**	**Fused (run-on) sentence**
mm	**9.**	**Misplaced modifier**
prep	**10.**	**Wrong or missing preposition**
ref	**11.**	**Unclear pronoun reference**
shift	**12.**	**Shift**
	12a.	Inappropriate shift in tense
	12b.	Inappropriate shift in pronoun
verb	**13.**	**Verb**
	13a.	Wrong or missing verb ending
	13b.	Wrong tense
	13c.	Wrong verb form
ww	**14.**	**Wrong word**

FIXING THE PROBLEMS

1. Comma ,

1a. Missing comma with an introductory element
Introductory words, phrases, or clauses are usually set off from the main clause of a sentence by a comma.

> Frankly, some members of my group did not do their share.
> After landing in New York, my grandfather settled in Wisconsin.

Although Thao arrived in the United States only three years ago, she gets top grades in English.

1b. Missing comma in a compound sentence

Place a comma before the coordinating conjunction joining the independent clauses in a compound sentence.

Michael spent the day writing letters to his girlfriend, and his grades showed it.

1c. Missing comma in a series

The widely accepted rule is to place a comma after each item in a series, including the next to last one before the final conjunction, usually *and.* Many newspapers do not follow this rule, but it makes sense if punctuation is intended to help the reader follow sentences accurately.

He cooked, danced, and joked his way into her heart.
My retired father fills his day by working in his garden, volunteering at his church, and following my mother around.
For breakfast, I like coffee, bacon and eggs, and toast.

1d. Missing comma(s) with nonrestrictive phrase or clause

A nonrestrictive phrase or clause modifies a noun but does not distinguish it from similar things it might be referring to. It should be set off with commas. (Contrast this with restrictive phrases or clauses.)

Abraham Lincoln, **citing his oath to defend the Union,** warned the South not to secede.
Thieves stole my computer, **which I need for my studies.**

1e. Incorrect comma(s) with restrictive element

A restrictive phrase or clause follows a noun and distinguishes it from similar things it might be referring to. It should not be set off with commas.

Incorrect commas: Students, **registering early,** get a better choice of classes.

Registering early is necessary to distinguish students registering early from other students; therefore, the phrase is restrictive and should not be set off with commas.

Better: Students **registering early** get a better choice of classes.

Incorrect commas: State troopers stop trucks, **which do not display their weight limits.**

Better: State troopers stop trucks **which** [or **that**] **do not display their weight limits.**

1f. Incorrect comma after is, was, *or other forms of the verb* be

In speaking, we sometimes pause momentarily after these verbs, especially when they are followed by *that* introducing a noun clause. Such a clause is a subject complement of the verb and should not be set off by a comma.

Incorrect comma: The problem with promising to attack immorality in America is, that people have such different ideas of where immorality lies.

Better: The problem with promising to attack immorality in America is that people have such different ideas of where immorality lies.

Semicolon ;

2a. Missing semicolon before however, therefore, *or another conjunctive adverb in a compound sentence*

This is a common form of comma splice (see **Comma splice**). Conjunctive adverbs are not like coordinating conjunctions and cannot be used to join the clauses in a compound sentence. A semicolon is the best way to solve this problem.

From DNA gathered on the scene, police have a complete genetic profile of the suspect; **however,** they do not know his name.

2b. Incorrect semicolon setting off phrases and dependent clauses

Generally, you are safest reserving semicolons to set off either independent clauses or items in a series when each item has internal commas. So unless you have a series with internal commas, use a comma rather than a semicolon to set off an item that cannot stand alone as a sentence.

Incorrect semicolon: The lawyers filed one appeal after another up through the court system; prolonging the case for over three years.

Better: The lawyers filed one appeal after another up through the court system, prolonging the case for over three years.

3. Apostrophe ’

3a. Missing or misplaced possessive apostrophe
Singular nouns are made possessive by the addition of *-'s*. In most cases, this is true even if the singular noun ends in *s*.

> The **song's** lyrics appalled **Karenna's** mother.
> The **class's** focus was on **Jesus's** teachings.

If the extra *s* sounds too awkward to you, you can use an *of* prepositional phrase (*the teachings of Jesus*) or an apostrophe alone (*the Dodgers' hometown, the Rams' quarterback*).

Most plural nouns are made possessive by the addition of an apostrophe after the plural *s* (*-s'*). If the plural noun does not end in *s*, add *-'s*.

> The **books'** covers had all been removed.
> The **children's** laughter echoed across the park.

If there are two or more nouns and you wish to indicate separate possession, add *-'s* to each one; if you wish to indicate joint possession, add *-'s* only to the last one.

> **Mario's** and **Kenny's** bikes were both stolen.
> **Dave and Laurie's** house looks beautiful.

3b. Its/it's confusion
Because apostrophes can indicate both a missing letter in contractions and possession, the use of *its* and *it's* can be confusing. In *it's*, the apostrophe indicates a missing letter, so *it's* is a shortened form of *it is*. *Its* is a possessive personal pronoun. Unlike nouns, which use an apostrophe in written English to show possession, personal pronouns have special possessive forms—*her, his, their, your, our,* and *its*.

> The dog ate **its** own lunch before it ate the cat's lunch.
> **It's** about time for the American public to start voting on election days.

4. Agreement agr

4a. Lack of subject-verb agreement
Subjects and verbs must agree in number; singular subjects go with singular verbs (*a horse gallops*), and plural subjects go with plural verbs (*many horses gallop*). Lack of agreement usually occurs when the subject and verb are

separated and we make the verb agree with a noun that is closer to it but is not the subject; often that noun is in a prepositional phrase such as *of the feud.* In the following example—*origins,* not *feud,* is the subject.

> The *origins* of the feud ~~lies~~ **lie** far in the past.

Care must be taken to make the subject agree with the verb when their normal order is reversed, as in the pattern beginning with the expletive *There.*

> There **are** twelve *apples* in the bowl.
> There **is** a *spider* at the bottom of the cup.

Compound subjects joined by *and* take plural verbs.

> *Jerry and Beth* **walk** together every day.

Compound subjects joined by *or, either . . . or,* or *neither . . . nor* may take singular verbs unless each subject is itself plural.

> Each day, *either Tom or Deborah* **looks** in on the invalid next door.
> *Either the neighbors or some family members* **weed** his garden every week.

Sometimes, a prepositional phrase such as *together with* may seem to set up a compound subject, but only conjunctions can do that; thus there is only a single subject for the verb to agree with in the following sentence.

> An army *colonel,* together with two assistants, **oversees** the distribution of food in the region.

4b. Lack of pronoun-antecedent agreement

Pronouns are words such as *I, you, he, she, it, we, they, me, him, her, them, my, his,* and *their.* They are noun substitutes and typically refer to nouns used earlier in writing or speech. The nouns they refer to are called their antecedents.

> *antecedent* *pronoun*
> A **truck** was ahead of me, and I could not see around **it.**

Pronouns must agree in number and gender with their antecedents. With a singular antecedent use a singular pronoun (*truck . . . it*), with a plural antecedent a plural pronoun (*trucks . . . they*); with a masculine antecedent use a masculine pronoun (*the prince . . . he*), with a feminine antecedent a feminine pronoun (*the princess . . . she*). Problems can arise in the following cases.

i. Compound antecedents normally take plural pronouns (*My* ***roommate and I*** *discussed what was bothering* ***us.***) but not when they are preceded by *every* or *each,* which are considered singular.

> **Every car** and **truck** must have ~~their~~ **its** engine checked for emissions.

ii. With gender, things can get even trickier. This is because most people have abandoned as sexist the old practice of using the masculine pronoun with singular or indefinite antecedents to stand for both males and females. In formal written English, the best solution is to use two singular pronouns.

> **Every student** must have ~~his~~ **his or her** picture taken.
> **Anyone** who parks in my space will wish ~~he~~ **he or she** hadn't.

Perhaps because of the awkwardness of writing and saying *his or her* and *he or she* all the time, more and more people are simply using the plural *their* and *they* in such cases, especially when speaking. This practice is probably on its way to becoming acceptable in formal writing, but it is not fully acceptable yet.

iii. Sometimes the antecedents of pronouns are not nouns but indefinite pronouns such as *each, either, neither,* and *one,* often followed by a prepositional phrase beginning with *of.* These are singular, and they (not the object of the preposition) must take singular pronouns.

> **Each** of my three uncles asked me to visit ~~them~~ **him** this summer.

5. Comma splice **cs**

A comma splice occurs when two independent clauses have only a comma separating them. An independent clause must either have end punctuation (a period, an exclamation point, or a question mark) or be joined to another independent clause by a comma plus a coordinating conjunction such as *and* or *but,* or by a semicolon. A comma alone is not enough. As with the run-on sentence, a comma splice often occurs when the writer senses a close relationship between the two independent clauses, so a semicolon is often a good fix for the comma splice.

> *Comma splice:* The Internet has made shopping from one's home very convenient, some people never go to a store any more.

Three possible revisions:
The Internet has made shopping from one's home very convenient, **and** [or **so**] some people never go to a store any more.
The Internet has made shopping from one's home very convenient**;** some people never go to a store any more.
The Internet has made shopping from one's home very convenient**.** **S**ome people never go to a store any more.

6. Dangling modifier **dm**

Dangling modifiers are usually participle or infinitive phrases that do not clearly modify a word in the sentence; sometimes there isn't even a word present for them to modify. Here are two examples.

Dangling participle phrase: **Fearing mudslides,** new building regulations were passed.

There's no word in the sentence that can act as the subject of *fearing mudslides*—nobody is doing the fearing.

Better: **Fearing mudslides,** the building **department** passed new regulations.

The subject of the sentence, *department,* can be interpreted as the subject of *Fearing mudslides*—this group of people is doing the fearing.

Dangling infinitive phrase: **In order to swim the channel,** a boat must be with a swimmer at all times.

The infinitive phrase cannot logically have the subject *boat* because a boat cannot swim.

Revised: **In order to swim the channel,** a **swimmer** must be accompanied by a boat at all times.

The subject of the revised sentence, swimmer, can logically perform the action in the infinitive phrase.

7. Fragment **frag**

A fragment is any structure that does not contain an independent clause and is punctuated as a sentence—with a capital letter at the beginning and a period at the end. For the most part, fragments should be eliminated from written English. Definitely, dependent clauses and participle phrases should be connected to an independent clause and not be punctuated as if they were sentences.

Fragment: Helena grabbed her coat and a pop tart. **Rushing to catch the bus.**

Revised: Helena grabbed her coat and a pop tart, **rushing to catch the bus.**

Fragment: **When the frozen mastodon was found with even its hair intact.** Scientists were amazed.

Revised: **When the frozen mastodon was found with even its hair intact,** scientists were amazed.

8. Fused (run-on) sentence **fs**

The fused sentence, also called the run-on sentence, occurs when we write two independent clauses and put no punctuation between them. Independent clauses must have a period (or another end punctuation such as a question mark or an exclamation mark), a semicolon, or a comma plus a coordinating conjunction between them. When we speak, we do not need to bother with punctuation, so we do not consciously notice when we end one independent clause and begin another; we make the point of conjunction clear with a pause and a drop in the pitch of our voice (or a rise if there is a question). However, we must pay attention to such things when we write or we confuse the reader. We often write a run-on sentence when we notice a close relationship between the two independent clauses, so a good fix for the run-on sentence is either a comma plus a coordinating conjunction or a semicolon. But a run-on sentence can also be fixed with end punctuation or even a dependent clause.

Fused: The earthquake crumbled some areas of the city the Capitol building was demolished.

Revised: The earthquake crumbled some areas of the city; the Capitol building was demolished.

or

The earthquake crumbled some areas of the city. **The** Capitol building was demolished.

Fused: Katerina looked for the phone book Abdul looked for the telephone.

Revised: Katerina looked for the phone book, **and** Abdul looked for the telephone.

or

Katerina looked for the phone book; Abdul looked for the telephone.

or

Katerina looked for the phone book **while** Abdul looked for the telephone.

9. Misplaced modifier mm

Because English is a word-order language, the placement of all words and phrases in a sentence can be very important for meaning, for clarity, and even for sense. We have discussed the placement of structures in nearly every chapter of this book; here is another example.

The princess was accompanied by the queen **who needed a chaperone.**

The princess, **who needed a chaperone,** was accompanied by the queen.

10. Wrong or missing preposition prep

Prepositions are word or word combinations such as *in, on, with, during, in regard to,* and *on behalf of* that indicate the relation of a noun or noun substitute (the object of the preposition) to another word in the sentence. People for whom English is a second language may have trouble choosing the right preposition or remembering to put one in. Native speakers of English correctly use prepositions all the time without having to think about them. This is amazing because prepositions appear in hundreds of different word combinations. Many of these are hard to explain—why do you log *on* and not *in* to the Internet? why are you guilty *of* a crime but blamed *for* a crime?—but they are also important. It makes a big difference whether you laugh *at* someone or *with* someone. And even when it doesn't make a big difference in meaning, a non-idiomatic prepositional phrase such as ∅*in the beach* will disturb your reader's attention; so will a missing preposition as in ∅*I will reply your letter.* If you are at all unsure about your prepositions, a good ESL textbook is the best reference work to consult; a good dictionary is useful, too. Here are a few examples of the kind of distinctions that give people trouble.

engaged to a person	absence from a class
engaged in an activity	absence of interest
engaged with a topic	make an alarm go off
fight against something	make an alarm go on
fight for something	

11. Unclear pronoun reference **ref**

Common pronouns include *I, you, he, she, it, we, they, her, him, them, this,* and *that.* They are noun substitutes; we use them instead of repeating nouns or ideas mentioned earlier. But it must always be clear exactly what or whom they refer to. This can be challenging, especially when there is more than one possibility. In such cases, it is better to repeat nouns than to risk vagueness or ambiguity in pronoun reference.

> *Unclear pronoun:* We will now have a chance to find out if charter schools can outperform public schools when efforts are made to improve **them.**
>
> *Better:* We will now have a chance to find out if charter schools can outperform public schools when efforts are made to improve **the public schools.**
>
> *Unclear pronoun:* During the 1960s, many American college students joined in demonstrations against the Vietnam War; during the same period many students also joined in civil rights demonstrations. **This** fact surprised the media.
>
> *Better:* During the 1960s, many American college students joined in demonstrations against the Vietnam War; during the same period many students also joined in civil rights demonstrations. **That they were equally engaged with both issues** surprised the media.

12. Shift **shift**

12a. Inappropriate shift in tense

The tenses of English are used fairly precisely in the standard dialect. We need to be careful not to shift the tense of verbs unnecessarily within a sentence or paragraph. This can sometimes be tricky when we are talking about events in the past (we ordinarily use the past tense to describe these), but then realize that we are still doing that thing in the present (we use simple present to describe such habitual actions). When faced with this dilemma in writing, we sometimes have to alter the facts so that we don't confuse the reader with a shift in tense. We also need to be sure that we do not shift from the past to the present by mistake.

Tense shift: I **wrote** to my mother every day while I was in France; I **like** to describe the meals that I **ordered,** and she **enjoys** reading about them.

Better: I **wrote** to my mother every day while I was in France; I **liked** to describe the meals that I **ordered,** and she **enjoyed** reading about them.

Tense shift: Clarissa **walked** to the window of her flat. She **looks** out into Hobart Square.

Better: Clarissa **walked** to the window of her flat. She **looked** out into Hobart Square.

12b. Inappropriate shift in pronoun

Do not make unnecessary and therefore confusing shifts in pronouns in your writing. Sometimes we start out thinking about things in one way and then change as we go on. Be sure to clean up these problem spots in your final writing.

Pronoun shift: If **one** drinks water from a polluted stream, **you** are likely to get sick.

Revised: If **you** drink water from a polluted stream, **you** are likely to get sick.

Pronoun shift: If my husband and I had eaten raw shrimp in Japan, **one** could have gotten very sick.

Revised: If my husband and I had eaten raw shrimp in Japan, **we** could have gotten very sick.

13. Verb **verb**

13a. Wrong or missing verb ending

ESL speakers and speakers of some dialects of English tend to omit the final *-s* where it is needed to make a present tense. The *-ed* ending is also often omitted when a past tense or past participle is needed. Even though these may seem small unnecessary things, they do indicate your ability to work well with standard English and are therefore important to get right, both in writing and in speaking.

> *Wrong ending:* Rosario **could** not **believes** her phone bill.
>
> *Revised:* Rosario **could** not **believe** her phone bill.
>
> *Missing ending:* Jerome **work** hard every day.
>
> *Revised:* Jerome **works** hard every day.
>
> *Missing ending:* Van **has look** for his missing essay for four days.
>
> *Revised:* Van **has looked** for his missing essay for four days.

13b. Wrong tense

The tenses of English are used fairly precisely in standard dialect, and we need to be sure that we are using the tense needed.

> *Wrong tense:* I **worked** six hours so far this week.
>
> *Revised:* I **have worked** six hours so far this week.
>
> *Wrong tense:* Hank **is** in Seattle for six days now.
>
> *Revised:* Hank **has been** in Seattle for six days now.
>
> *Wrong tense:* After I **will finish** washing the car, I **will clean** the house.
>
> *Revised:* After I **finish** washing the car, I **will clean** the house.

13c. Wrong verb form

Because English has some irregular verbs that do not use the *-ed* suffix to make their past tense and past participle and because some dialects of English do not make their past tense and past participle in the standard way, we sometimes have problems with verb forms.

> *Wrong verb form:* Mr. Vasquez **had came** from Chile only three years before becoming manager of the company.
>
> *Revised:* Mr. Vasquez **had come** from Chile only three years before becoming manager of the company.
>
> *Wrong verb form:* Paul **brung** me vanilla beans from Tahiti.
> *Revised:* Paul **brought** me vanilla beans from Tahiti.

14. Wrong word **ww**

There are many words in English that, although not homonyms, still sound a lot alike. So sometimes we make the mistake of using one when we should be using the other. Other times, words that really do not exist are used because they sound like real words. Sometimes we actually have learned a wrong word from people around us, other times we are reaching a little beyond our securely learned vocabulary and make an error, and still other times we have misheard a word. We need to stay perpetually alert to avoid these mistakes.

Wrong word: Jolene was involved in many **incidences** involving the police.

Right word: Jolene was involved in many **incidents** involving the police.

Wrong word: Do you **ascribe** to the idea that our state of mind causes our physical illnesses?

Right word: Do you **subscribe** to the idea that our state of mind causes our physical illnesses?

Wrong word: People who own big diamonds sometimes **flout** them.

Right word: People who own big diamonds sometimes **flaunt** them.

Wrong word: He openly **flaunted** the law.

Right word: He openly **flouted** the law.

Wrong word: The difficulty of getting Republicans and Democrats to agree on a solution **mitigates against** solving the Social Security problem.

Right word: The difficulty of getting Republicans and Democrats to agree on a solution **militates against** solving the Social Security problem.

Wrong word: I wonder how those weeds **promulgate** themselves.

Right word: I wonder how those weeds **propagate** themselves.

APPENDIX B

PARTS OF SPEECH

FORM CLASSES

The information here applies to prototypical members of each word class—those that display the basic characteristics of form and function that belong to the class. **Form** refers to the outer shape of a word—mainly how it is spelled and pronounced. **Function** refers to what words can do in sentences and where they can go in relation to other words. Form and function are better guides than meaning to which part of speech a word represents. A word usually has to meet some combination of formal and/or functional criteria (or "proofs") to be considered a certain part of speech. The four form classes—noun, verb, adjective, and adverb—are so called because they undergo changes in form, such as the addition of *-s* to indicate plural or *-ed* to indicate past tense. These classes contain most of the words in English. They are called "open" classes because new words are continually being added to them.

Part of Speech	*Sentence Functions and Examples*	*Formal Proofs*	*Functional Proofs*
Nouns	Are subjects and objects (direct, indirect, object of preposition) and other kinds of complements (subject comp., object comp.). The *name* of the *student* in the first *row* is *Kit Cruz.* Her *intelligence* and hard *work* have earned her a *grant* from the *Ford Foundation.*	Can be made plural, usually by adding *-s* (count nouns). Can be made possessive by adding *-'s.* Often have suffixes such as *-ence, -ship, -tion,* and *-ism,* indicating derivation from other words.	Can directly follow determiners such as *the, a/an, this,* and *my* to form a grammatical unit. Fit into frame sentence: (The) ________ seems important (fine, unavoidable).* *Honesty* seems important.
Common	Count: *name, student, row, grant* Noncount: *intelligence, work*		
Proper	*Kit Cruz, Ford Foundation*		
Verbs	Function in predicates, making statements about subjects. People *criticize* Brian, but I *admire* him. He *takes* risks and *invests* in good ideas. Last year he *invested* in an espresso cart, and now he *is making* lots of money and *has* even *given* some to charitable causes.	Add *-s* for third-person singular: He (She, It) *takes.* Change form to show past tense (*invested*), past participle (*given*), and present participle (*making*). Often have prefixes and suffixes such as *dis-, -ate, -ize,* indicating derivation from other words.	Can be negated: I *did not walk.* Often can be made into a command: *Invest!* Can take auxiliaries such as *be, have, must, might, would, could, should, may.* Fit into frame sentence: We should ________ (it).

Adjectives	Modify nouns or function as complements of nouns; often answer the questions which? and what kind of? In the *furious* rain, a *tall* man and a *short* man shared a *small, collapsible* umbrella. The *tall* man looked *unhappy;* he was not *collapsible.*	Often have characteristic adjective endings such as *-ous, -able, -ible, -ish, -ful,* and *-ive: collapsible, enormous, contagious, lovable, childish, masterful.* Can be compared using the suffixes *-er* and *-est,* or *more* and *most: tall, taller, tallest.*	Can follow qualifiers such as *very, rather, somewhat, fairly.* Fit into both slots of the frame sentence: The ________ dog is very ________.
Adverbs	Modify verbs; typically answer the questions how? when? where? why? and to what extent? *Tightly* clutching the roses, his heart beating *fast,* Archie rang the doorbell. The door opened *immediately,* and *soon* an Irish Setter was *avidly* licking his face.	Commonly include the suffix *-ly,* and sometimes *-wise, -ward,* and *-ways* (*lengthwise, upward*). Some can be compared using *-er* and *-est,* or *more* and *most: fast, faster, fastest.*†	Can take qualifiers such as *very, rather, somewhat, fairly, too.* Can often be moved within a sentence: *Softly,* the snow fell. The snow fell *softly.* Fit into frame sentence: He read the letter ________.

*Parentheses around *The* indicate it is optional. In all frame sentences, some words may need to be changed for the sentence to make sense.
†Words like *fast* (or *slow*) can be both adjectives and adverbs.

Structure Classes

The structure classes help set up the structural relations among words, phrases, clauses, and sentences. The structure classes are considered closed—new words are not added to them. Although some structure classes—especially pronouns—may undergo form changes, most do not.

Part of Speech	*Subclasses and Examples*		*Sentence Functions and Characteristics*
Pronouns	*I* called Al and offered *him* a job *that* pays more than *mine* pays.		Substitute for nouns or for phrases that fill noun slots.
	Subject Case	Object Case	In subject case function in clauses as subjects or subject complements. In object case function as direct objects, indirect objects, objects of prepositions, and subjects in infinitive phrases.
Personal	*I, you, he, she, it, we, you, they*	*me, you, him, her, it, us, you, them*	
Relative	*who, which, that, what*	*whom, which, that, what*	
Interrogative	*who, which, what*	*whom, which, what*	
	Pronouns that function as both subject/subject complement and object:		
Possessive	*mine, yours, his, hers, its, ours, yours, theirs*		Possessive pronouns can function as both nouns and as determiners.
Indefinite	*any, anyone, another, one, none, each, everyone, others, many, and so on*		
Demonstrative	*this, that, these, those*		
Reflexive/ Emphatic*	*myself, yourself, himself, herself, itself, ourselves, yourselves*		
Auxiliaries†	I *must* visit my grandmother. I *have* not visited her for weeks because I *am* working two jobs and *do* not have any free time.		Precede or substitute for main verbs. When preceding a main verb, auxiliaries become part of the verb phrase and affect the meaning of the verb.
Modals	*can, could, may, might, must, shall, should, will, would*		
Be	*am, are, is, was, were*		
Have	*have, has, had*		
Do	*do, does, did*		

Determiners	*The* teacher gave *a* brief test over *the last five* chapters *this* week.	Signal that a noun is coming. Determiners modify the nouns they precede, helping to narrow their meaning, but differ from adjectives in important ways. Their normal position when adjectives are present is before the adjectives.
Articles	*the, a, an*	
Demonstratives	*this, these, that, those*	
Possessives	*my, our, your, his, her, its, their* (also possessive nouns: *Kate's, kids'*)	
Indefinites	*some, any, no, every, other, another, many, more, most, all, both*	
Cardinal numbers	*one, two, three, four,* and so on	
Ordinal numbers	*first, second, third . . . last*	
Qualifiers	It was *too* hot to play *even* a little tennis in the afternoon, but it became *quite* comfortable by evening. *very, quite, rather, somewhat, more, less, least, too, even, really,* and so on	Precede adjectives or adverbs to increase or decrease the quality they signify. Unlike adverbs, qualifiers cannot be moved or intensified.
Prepositions	Men *in* uniform marched *through* the streets. *According to* my sister, one *of* them was *out of* step. *about, above, at, before, behind, concerning, despite, during, for, in, into, like, near, of, out, over, past, since, to, and so on, according to, along with, because of, thanks to,* and so on	Always precede a noun (and its determiners and modifiers) to form a prepositional phrase.
Conjunctions	Al ordered steak, *and* I ordered salmon; *however,* the restaurant was out of *both* steak *and* salmon, *so* we left *because* nothing else on the menu appealed to *either* Al *or* me.	Coordinating and correlative conjunctions join words or structures that have identical functions, including independent clauses. Subordinating conjunctions introduce dependent clauses and
Coordinating	*and, but, for, nor, or, yet, so*	
Correlative	*both . . . and, either . . . or, neither . . . nor, not (only) . . . but (also)*	

Part of Speech	*Subclasses and Examples*	*Sentence Functions and Characteristics*
Subordinating	*because, since, after, as, as soon as, as if, if. more than*	connect them to other structures.
Conjunctive adverbs	*however, instead, nevertheless, also, accordingly, finally,* and so on	Conjunctive adverbs can help join independent clauses.
Expletives	*There* is no room (delayed subject) in the van. *It* is a pity that you can't join us. (delayed subject) *there, it*	Serve as placeholders for other words (usually delayed subjects).

*Reflexive nouns normally serve as objects (*I hurt* ***myself***), but can be subject complements: *I am not* ***myself.*** As emphatic pronouns, they can be appositives of subjects: *John* ***himself*** *came.*

†*Be, have,* and *do* also function as main verbs.

APPENDIX C

Basic Sentence Patterns

There are five to ten basic sentence patterns underlying almost all English sentences; grammarians differ on the exact number. We count eight. This chart labels the different slots that make each pattern. Each slot is labeled by function (for example, subject) and by the part of speech that typically performs this function (for example, noun). The sentences used here as examples are skeletal. In sentences people actually speak and write, the slots are often filled by phrases and clauses performing the functions of the single-word parts of speech, and the skeletons are fleshed out with modifiers. The chart shows only the slots that are obligatory for each pattern.

The verb is the pivotal slot in each pattern; it determines and controls the pattern. Look in the glossary for further explanations and examples of **intransitive verbs, linking verbs,** and **transitive verbs**.

		Predicate		
	Subject	*Verb*	*Complement*	*Complement*
Pattern 1	Subject **noun** *The children*	Intransitive verb **verb/intransitive** *play.*		
Pattern 2	Subject **noun** *The children*	*Be** **verb/*be*** *are*	Adverbial complement **adverb of time/place** *everywhere.*	
Pattern 3	Subject **noun 1** *The children*	Linking verb **verb/linking** *are*	Subject complement—adjective **adjective** *tireless.*	
Pattern 4	Subject **noun 1**† *The children*	Linking verb **verb/linking** *are*	Subject complement—noun **noun 1** *dynamos.*	
Pattern 5	Subject **noun 1** *The children*	Transitive verb **verb/transitive** *love*	Direct object **noun 2** *games.*	
Pattern 6	Subject **noun 1** *The children*	Transitive verb **verb/transitive** *give*	Indirect object **noun 2** *their teachers*	Direct object **noun 3** *pleasure.*

Pattern 7	Subject	Transitive verb	Direct object	Object complement—adjective
	noun 1	**verb/transitive**	**noun 2**	**adjective**
	The children	*consider*	*naps*	*unnecessary.*
Pattern 8	Subject	Transitive verb	Direct object	Object complement—noun
	noun 1	**verb/transitive**	**noun 2**	**noun 2**
	The children	*consider*	*naps*	*a nuisance.*

*Pattern 2 is the only pattern centered on a single verb—*be. Be* can also function as a linking verb in patterns 3 and 4. The forms of *be* are *am, is, are, was, were,* and the participles *being* and *been.*

†Numbers indicate whether the nouns in a sentence pattern refer to the same thing or to different things. In pattern 4, for example, *children* and *dynamos* refer to the same thing, with the linking verb functioning as an equal sign; thus both nouns are designated "noun 1." In pattern 6, each of the three nouns refers to a different thing; so the nouns are designated "noun 1," "noun 2," and "noun 3."

APPENDIX D

PRONOUN CHART

	*Subjective (Nominative)**		*Objective*†		*Possessive Pronouns*‡		*Possessive Adjectives (Determiners)*§	
	Singular	**Plural**	**Singular**	**Plural**	**Singular**	**Plural**	**Singular**	**Plural**
Personal	I	we	me	us	mine	ours	my	our
	you	you	you	you	yours	yours	your	your
	he	they	him	them	his	theirs	his	their
	she		her		hers		her	
	it		it		its		it	
	I threw the ball. *We* walked at dawn.		Mary called *me*. Rain ruined *them*.		*Mine* flew away. (subject) Alan took *theirs*. (object)		*My* car runs well. Birds ate *our* plums.	

	*Subjective (Nominative)**	*Objective*†	*Possessive Pronouns*‡	*Possessive Adjectives (Determiners)*§
Relative	**Singular and Plural**	**Singular and Plural**		**Singular and Plural**
	who which that what	whom which that what		whose
	People *who* laugh live long. Wool, *which* shrinks easily, must be carefully cleaned.	The student with *whom* I sat came from Iran. I don't care *which* you choose.		The man *whose* car I bought has disappeared.
Interrogative	**Singular and Plural**	**Singular and Plural**		**Singular and Plural**
	who which that what	whom which that what		whose
	Who built that house? *What* is wrong with you?	*Whom* will you invite to your party? *Which* do you prefer?		*Whose* book is that?

*Subjective pronouns function as subjects and subjective complements in independent and dependent clauses.
†Objective pronouns function as direct objects, indirect objects, objects of preposition, and subjects in infinitive phrases.
‡Possessive pronouns function as either subjects or objects. They replace the possessive adjective followed by a noun (*my* + noun = *mine*).
§Possessive adjective pronouns signal and modify nouns.

OTHER PRONOUN CLASSES

Demonstrative (both subjective and objective; no possessive form): *this, these, that,* and *those.*

> **This** is my box. I want **those**.

Indefinite (both subjective and objective; some form the possessive with apostrophe): *any, another, anyone, one, none, each, everyone,* and *others.*

> **One** must be careful. Be kind to **everyone**.

Reflexive (objective only): *myself, yourself, himself, herself, itself, ourselves, yourselves,* and *themselves.*

> I hurt **myself**. Take care of **yourselves**.

Intensive (functions as an appositive of the noun or pronoun): *myself, yourself, himself, herself, itself, ourselves, yourselves,* and *themselves.*

> George **himself** signed the letter. I insist on speaking to the President **himself**.

Answer Key

Chapter 1: A Few Things to Get Started

Parts of Speech: Form and Function

1. Sandy's *book* (noun) was published last month. She has *booked* (verb) tickets for a national tour.
2. I *met* (verb) with my last boss every month. I *meet* (verb) with my present boss every day.
3. There are many *theories* (noun) about whale songs. One *theory* (noun) is that they are mating calls.
4. Scientists have *mapped* (verb) the human genome. At this point, the *maps* (noun) are still crude.
5. Your last *fax* (noun) didn't come through. *Fax* (verb) it again.

Subjects and Verbs

1. The child reached U.S. shores alone. Subject: child; Verb: reached
2. Did you see the Beatles in a live concert? Subject: you; Verb: did see
3. Where were you during the storm? Subject: you; Verb: were
4. The package has arrived safely. Subject: package; Verb: has arrived
5. A dog did not dig that hole. Subject: dog; Verb: did dig

Sentences

Complete Subject	Predicate
1. Mary Lou	picked only the yellow flowers for the bouquet
2. The red fire engine	honked loudly at the intersection
3. Ten of the children	have had their measles shot already
4. Physics	is a hard but rewarding subject
5. Evolutionary biology	is used to study human psychology

Sentence Patterns

SUBJECT	VERB	DIRECT OBJECT
1. chef	stirred	ganache
2. winds	whipped	ocean
3. ice	cooled	forehead
4. student	interrupted	teacher
5. Shakespeare	wrote	tragedies

SUBJECT	VERB	SUBJECT COMPLEMENT
1. Lucy	was	lucky
2. Crowd	seemed	angry
3. Suit	was	color
4. That	is	weirdness
5. Alice	became	sleepy

Independent and Dependent Clauses

INDEPENDENT	DEPENDENT
1. Nell swam to the shore	after her canoe capsized
2. Einstein is the person	who recognized time as the fourth dimension
3. the scientists at Los Alamos worked in their labs	While the war raged
4. the snow melts	When Chinook winds sweep down the mountains
5. you want the next batter to be good	When the bases are loaded

Fragments

1. When DNA was discovered. *fragment*
2. Yoga is commonly suggested as a stress reliever.
3. Leaning into the wind. *fragment*
4. During the sociology class. *fragment*
5. Mothers know when their children need them.

Active and Passive Voice

1. The drunk driver was arrested (*passive*) shortly after leaving the scene of the accident.
2. The arresting officer read him his Miranda rights.
3. Qualifying for the Olympics is a major victory.
4. Since DNA was discovered (*passive*), huge advances in biology have occurred.
5. The swelling caused great pain. The pain was relieved (*passive*) by the cold compress.

Chapter 2: Modification

Modifiers of Nouns: Adjectives and Adjectivals
Note: Adjectives and adjectivals are <u>underlined</u>; nouns are in **boldface.** *In all case, the adjectives precede the nouns they modify.*

1. <u>The</u> <u>high</u> **seas** began to cause <u>grave</u> **concern** among <u>the</u> <u>ship's</u> **crew.**
2. <u>The</u> <u>gathering</u> **storm** would reach them in <u>a</u> <u>few</u> **minutes.**
3. <u>Whale</u> **blubber** had <u>many</u> **uses** in <u>the</u> <u>nineteenth</u> **century.**
4. <u>Fossil</u> **fuels** were just being developed for <u>home</u> and <u>industrial</u> **use.**
5. Today, <u>many</u> **people** consider whales <u>beautiful,</u> <u>complex</u> **creatures.**

Modifiers of Verbs: Adverbs and Adverbial Structures
Note: Adverbs are <u>underlined</u>; verbs are in **boldface.** *In all cases, the adverbs modify the verb in the same clause.*

1. The liner **moved** <u>slowly</u> <u>away</u> as family members <u>tearfully</u> **waved** good-bye.
2. <u>Soon</u> the liner **would enter** dangerous waters.
3. Enemy submarines **were** <u>then</u> <u>stealthily</u> **patrolling** the waters beyond the harbor.
4. Those who stayed home **would** <u>not</u> <u>always</u> **be** safe.
5. Crossing the ocean <u>usually</u> **involved** less risk.

Modifiers of Adjectives and Adverbs: Qualifiers
Note: Qualifiers are <u>underlined</u>; the words they modify are in **boldface** *and followed by (adj.) if adjective or (adv.) if adverb.*

1. People with <u>very</u> **pale** *(adj.)* skin should wear sunblock <u>almost</u> **daily** *(adv.)*.
2. They should apply it <u>very</u> **carefully** *(adv.)* to all exposed parts of their bodies.
3. Yesterday, it was <u>too</u> **hot** *(adj.)* to play <u>even</u> a **little** *(adj.)* tennis.
4. I was interested in <u>more</u> **sedentary** *(adj.)* activities.
5. By evening, it had become <u>quite</u> **comfortable** *(adj.)*.

Placement of Modifiers
Note: = indicates where the modifier could go in each sentence; sometimes there is more than one possible place.

1. (noisily) = The children = came = back = to the classroom from recess.
2. (messy) A = roommate can be very difficult to live with.
3. (surprise) Lena loves to give = birthday parties.
4. (carefully) Because he did not want to disturb any evidence, the detective = inspected the scene of the crime =.
5. (careful) The =, skillful, = surgeon cut through fat and muscle to reach the stomach.

Prepositional Phrases

Prepositional phrase	Word modified
1. After the long hike	ate
with gusto	ate
2. on emissions	controls
from all gasoline engines	emissions
3. Outside the theater	waited
in line	waited
for tickets	waited

4. on my right	man
like a baby	slept
during the flight	slept
5. of whales	songs
of beauty and variety	full
in subtle ways	change
over the course	change
of a mating season	course

Chapter 3: Appositives

A. Practicing Sentence Combining
Note: For all the sentence combining exercises in the book, there are some cases in which variations other than those given in this answer key are possible.

1. Art Tatum, one of the great jazz pianists of the century, was completely blind.
   or
   One of the great jazz pianists of the century, Art Tatum, was blind from birth.
   or
   One of the great jazz pianists of the century Art Tatum, was blind from birth.
2. In 1996, world chess champion Gary Kasparov accepted the challenge of playing against IBM's Deep Blue, a powerful chess-playing computer program.
   or
   In 1996, Gary Kasparov, world chess champion, accepted the challenge of playing against IBM's Deep Blue, a powerful chess-playing computer program.
3. Erwin Shrödinger thought life was governed by a "genetic code," a phrase he coined.
4. A collector of rare wine, Arthur wanted a house with a cool, dry cellar.
   or
   Arthur, a collector of rare wine, wanted a house with a cool, dry cellar.

5. Michael Jordan was a master of every kind of shot—three pointers, slam dunks, free throws.
   or
   Three pointers, slam dunks, free throws—Michael Jordan was a master of every kind of shot.
6. The San Antonio Spurs's Tim Duncan is being called "the Air apparent," a pun suggesting he may be the next Michael "Air" Jordan.
7. Yoga for kids, an outgrowth of the latest adult trend, is a burgeoning industry.
   or
   An outgrowth of the latest adult trend, yoga for kids is a burgeoning industry.
8. A walk around the block with little Chloe is a joy, a voyage of discovery led by a tireless explorer.
9. Florence is full of great sculptures of the young David, the symbol of young, upstart Florence challenging the power of Goliath Rome.
10. New regulations will create three categories of sunburn protection: "minimal" (SPF 2 to 12), "moderate" (12 to 30), and "high" (30 and more).
11. The Maya, an Amerindian people who flourished between 300 and 800 C.E., left pyramids and monuments that are among the wonders of the world.
12. Their architectural and engineering achievements—astonishing pyramids, palaces, and bas-reliefs—are found at several sites in Central America.
13. The major sites, Uxmal, Uxactum, Copán, Piedras, and Tixal, are in northern Guatemala and southern Mexico.
14. The largest site, Tixal, may have had a population of 40,000 people.
15. One archeologist, Dr. Richard D. Hansen, a professor at UCLA, believes the Maya may have brought ecological disaster upon themselves.
16. Lime stucco, the material used in much Maya architecture, is made by melting limestone.
17. The melting of the limestone, a process that requires intense heat, led to the leveling of forests for firewood.

18. Dr. Hansen suggests that deforestation, a major cause of soil erosion, destroyed the seasonal swamps where the Maya had been collecting peat to fertilize their terraced agricultural gardens.
19. Dr. David Friedel, another speaker at the conference where Dr. Hansen presented his theory, said Dr. Hansen's theory was convincing only when applied to the area of northern Guatemala where Dr. Hansen had been working.
20. For the general collapse of the Maya civilization, other causes—population pressure on the agricultural system, constant warfare, changing trade routes, drought and other climactic factors, and competition among elites—may have been more important.

C. Appositives in Published Writing
From Diane Ackerman, *The Moon by Whale Light and Other Adventures among Bats, Penguins, Crocodilians, and Whales* (New York: Random House, 1991), 115; appositives in **boldface.**

> If you ask someone to draw a whale, she will probably draw a sperm whale, **the bulbous-headed whale made famous in Melville's *Moby Dick,* a book that is as much a treatise on whales as it is a piece of fiction.** But whales come in many shapes, sizes, and colors. There are two basic groups: **the toothed whales (Odontoceti, from the Latin for "tooth" and "whale")** and **the baleen whales (Mysticeti, from the Latinized Greek word for "whale").**

D. Combining in Context
Note: Appositives are in **boldface.**

1. The origins of the Koran, **the sacred book of Islam,** have been undergoing reexamination by Muslim and non-Muslim scholars around the world. The traditional belief **that the Koran is the actual Word of God as revealed to the prophet Muhammad** is still widely adhered to within Islam. According to this belief, the illiterate Muhammad received his revelations from the angel Gabriel and then reported them verbatim to family members and friends, who either memorized them or wrote them down. About fifteen years after Muhammad's death, Caliph 'Uthman, **the third Islamic ruler to succeed Muhammad,** became concerned over the growth of Islamic sects claiming differing versions

of the Koranic scripture. He ordered a committee to gather the various pieces of scripture into one standard written version; all incomplete and "imperfect" collections were destroyed. Some modern scholars think this is an example of "salvation history," **a story about a religion's origins invented later and projected back in time for religious purposes.** These scholars think that the Koran, like the Bible, may be a compilation of oral and written traditions from many sources.

2. Mihaly Csikszentmihalyi, **a professor of psychology at the University of Chicago,** is an authority on "flow" experiences. In one of his books, ***Flow,*** he describes flow experiences as moments of intense living when "what we feel, what we wish, and what we think are in harmony." He identifies several conditions that are usually present in such experiences: **clear goals, immediate feedback,** and—perhaps most important—**balance between challenge and skills.** He writes, "Flow tends to occur when a person's skills are fully involved in overcoming a challenge that is just about manageable." Some activities—**climbing a mountain, playing a musical piece, performing surgery**—are highly likely to furnish flow experiences to those who engage in them. Finding flow in everyday life is harder but possible, according to Csikszentmihalyi. **An energetic optimist,** he believes people can take conscious steps to find flow both at work and at home and that doing so could significantly improve the lives of many people.

Chapter 4: Appositive Adjectives

A. Practicing Sentence Combining

1. Huge and savage, the waves battered the beach.

   or

   The waves, huge and savage, battered the beach.

2. New and shiny, a sports car sat in the driveway.

   or

   A sports car, new and shiny, sat in the driveway.

   or

   A sports car sat in the driveway, new and shiny.

3. Loud and relentlessly competitive, the new music student from Los Angeles became instantly unpopular with almost everybody in the class.

or

The new music student from Los Angeles, loud and relentlessly competitive, became instantly unpopular with almost everybody in the class.

4. Short but imposing, the secretary of state attracted attention whenever she entered a room.

   or

   The secretary of state, short but imposing, attracted attention whenever she entered a room.

5. Willful and proud, Oedipus is sure he will beat the oracle's prediction.

   or

   Oedipus, willful and proud, is sure he will beat the oracle's prediction.

6. Green and inviting, the clean ocean water was a rich reward for the long hike.

   or

   The clean ocean water, green and inviting, was a rich reward for the long hike.

7. Strict, demanding, but kind, the drama teacher eventually won the devotion of all her students.

   or

   The drama teacher, strict and demanding but kind, eventually won the devotion of all her students.

8. Hot and wonderfully crusty, the French bread went perfectly with the soup.

   or

   The French bread, hot and wonderfully crusty, went perfectly with the soup.

9. Economically simple but socially complex, the African pygmy tribe was fascinating to study.

   or

   The African pygmy tribe, economically simple but socially complex, was fascinating to study.

10. Dark and moist, Cliff's brownies were the first item to sell out at the bake sale.

    or

    Cliff's brownies, dark and moist, were the first item to sell out at the bake sale

11. Long and demanding, Richard Wagner's opera *Tristan and Isolde* amply rewards the listener who can get past the intricate, farfetched plot.
    or
    Richard Wagner's opera *Tristan and Isolde,* long and demanding, amply rewards the listener who can get past the intricate, farfetched plot.
12. Profoundly loyal and dutiful, Tristan is bringing Isolde from Ireland to be the bride of his uncle, King Marke of Cornwall.
    or
    Tristan, profoundly loyal and dutiful, is bringing Isolde from Ireland to be the bride of his uncle, King Marke of Cornwall.
13. Proud and haughty, Isolde is the daughter of a line of mighty sorcerers.
    or
    Isolde, proud and haughty, is the daughter of a line of mighty sorcerers.
14. Half in love with Tristan from an earlier encounter but furious at him for having captured her for King Marke, Isolde prepares a poison mixture with which to kill both Tristan and herself.
    or
    Isolde, both half in love with Tristan from an earlier encounter and furious at him for having captured her for King Marke, prepares a poison mixture with which to kill both Tristan and herself.
15. Well-meaning but shortsighted, her servant substitutes a love potion for the poison mixture, and Tristan and Isolde drink it.
    or
    Her servant, well-meaning but shortsighted, substitutes a love potion for the poison mixture, and Tristan and Isolde drink it.
16. Helplessly in love, Tristan and Isolde rush into one another's arms, aware that their love is doomed.
    or
    Tristan and Isolde, helplessly in love but aware that their love is doomed, rush into one another's arms.
17. Oblivious of everything around them, Tristan and Isolde pour out their love for each other as their ship docks in Cornwall and King Marke prepares to board.
    or
    Tristan and Isolde, oblivious of everything around them, pour out their love for each other as their ship docks in Cornwall and King Marke prepares to board.

18. Almost embarrassing in its sensuality, the music of their long love scene rises by slow chromatic steps to an excruciatingly delayed climax.

    or

    The music of their long love scene, almost embarrassing in its sensuality, rises by slow chromatic steps to an excruciatingly delayed climax.
19. A series of misunderstandings, avoidable and thus all the more tragic, leads to Tristan's death from wounds inflicted by King Marke's lieutenant, Melot.
20. The love-scene music returns in the famous Liebestod ("love-death"), which Isolde sings over Tristan's body before, dead of a broken heart, she falls upon him.

    or

    The love-scene music returns in the famous Liebestod ("love-death"), which Isolde sings over Tristan's body before she falls upon him, dead of a broken heart.

C. Appositive Adjectives in Published Writing

From Ralph Ellison, "Remembering Jimmy," in *Shadow and Act* (New York: Signet Books, 1966), 235; appositive adjectives in **boldface.**

> In the old days, the voice was high and clear and poignantly lyrical. **Steel-bright in its upper range,** and, **at its best, silky smooth,** it was possessed of a purity somehow impervious to both the stress of singing above a twelve-piece band and the urgency of Rushing's own blazing fervor. On dance nights, when you stood on the rise of the school grounds two blocks to the east, you could hear it jetting from the dance hall like a blue flame in the dark.

D. Combining in Context

Note: Appositive adjectives are in **boldface.**

1. Cyril could not believe it was happening. All those empty seats in the Greyhound bus and this striking young woman chose the seat next to his. Every feature was perfect. Her abundant, jet-black hair came almost to her shoulders and then curled elegantly upward. Her eyes, **dark and mysterious,** were at the same time friendly. Her high, prominent cheekbones gave her face a regal look. Her nose, **delicate and shapely,** reminded him of the Song of Solomon. **Full and sensual,** her naturally red lips curved slightly upward in a permanent modest half-smile that

widened into a dazzling full smile as she asked, "Excuse me. May I sit here, or is this seat taken?" "No, I mean yes, I mean no," said Cyril, hating himself. His response brought a delighted musical laugh out of her throat. "I do that all the time, too," she said. This woman, **beautiful and also kind,** seemed to be everything Cyril had always dreamed of. He was in love.

2. **Japanese in origin but American in everything else,** the teenagers at the Manzanar internment camp in 1942 played touch football, tried out for cheerleading squads, and performed Glen Miller arrangements in their bands. They also took advantage of camp life to taste the freedom of American children. Mealtimes could no longer be traditional affairs around a table presided over by a patriarchal father. Camp residents ate at long tables in mess halls, and family members would scatter in search of mess halls with shorter lines or better food. The more ambitious ones would get second meals by moving between early servings at one mess hall and later ones at another. For the children, this was fun. For their fathers, **already angry and depressed,** it was another blow to their manly pride. According to Jeanne Wakatsuki Houston in *Farewell to Manzanar,* the final "snip of the castrator's scissors" came upon their return home from the camps. Her father found his car repossessed and his fishing boats gone without any records. **Impoverished and emasculated,** he never recovered his faith in himself or in the country to which he had come so full of energy and hope.

Chapter 5: Compound Sentences

A. Practicing Sentence Combining

1. It was the day before Valentine's Day, and [or *so*] the lines outside Fran's Chocolates stretched around the block.
2. The Mayor tried to have both freedom and order on the streets, but [or ;] he ended up having repression and chaos.
3. Orlando was a superb cook, and Julio was a superb gardener but [or ;] neither of them could bear to clean house.
4. The family was, as usual, evenly divided over vacation plans: Dad wanted to go to Maine, Mom wanted to go to the Jersey Shore, and Jesse wanted to go nowhere.
5. Solomon had no way of knowing who the real mother was, so [or *but*] he found a way of making her reveal herself.

6. Some people assumed F. Scott Fitzgerald was shallow and stupid, for they could not separate the author from his characters.
7. Not only is she a skilled administrator and a prizewinning poet; she is also an accomplished mountain climber and an expert mechanic.
   or
   Not only is she a skilled administrator and a prizewinning poet, but she is also an accomplished mountain climber and an expert mechanic.
8. On his first date, Rudy left nothing to chance; [or :] he even rented a car because his was unreliable.
9. According to Dostoevsky's Grand Inquisitor, people do not desire freedom; they desire bread, mystery, and authority.
10. Felix's mother was also his math teacher; however, she cut him no slack when marking his tests.
11. The class trip was supposed to include a visit to a volcano, but the visit was canceled.
12. Seismologists had recorded underground rumblings, and they advised against approaching the volcano.
13. Were the rumblings the voices of the gods, as some people believed, or were they merely the result of the underground movement of molten rock?
14. At its last eruption, the volcano created a river of melted snow, and this river swept seven people to their deaths.
15. The last eruption was in 1985, when I was ten years old, so it is only a vague memory for me.
16. Authorities warned people to clear the area, but many people were not very smart.
17. Good luck can save people from their own stupidity for a long time, but, in an emergency, their own stupidity will often catch up with them.
18. Gamblers think we live in a world where luck rules, and dreamers think we live in a world where wishing makes it so; they are both wrong.
19. Actions have consequences, and these [or *consequences*] must be considered before we take actions.
20. People who disregarded this truth ignored a clear warning, and the truth was brought home to them in a violent way.

C. Compound Sentences in Published Writing
From David Brooks, "The Organization Kid, *Atlantic Monthly,* April (2001), 40; compound sentences in **boldface.**

> In our conversations I would ask the [Princeton] students when they got around to sleeping. **One senior told me that she went to bed around two and woke up each morning at seven; she could afford that much rest because she had learned to supplement her full day of work by studying in her sleep. As she was falling asleep she would recite a math problem or a paper topic to herself; she would then sometimes dream about it, and when she woke up, the problem might be solved. I asked several students to describe their daily schedules, and their replies sounded like a session of future Workaholics of America: crew practice at dawn, classes in the morning, resident-adviser duty, lunch, study groups, classes in the afternoon, tutoring disadvantaged kids in Trenton, a cappella practice, dinner, study, science lab, prayer session, hit the StairMaster, study a few hours more.** One young man told me that he had to schedule appointment times for chatting with his friends. **I mentioned this to other groups, and usually one or two people would volunteer that they did the same thing.** "I just had an appointment with my best friend at seven this morning," one woman said. "Or else you lose touch."
>
> There are a lot of things these future leaders no longer have time for. **I was on campus at the height of the election season, and I saw not even one Bush or Gore poster.** I asked around about this and was told that most students have no time to read newspapers, follow national politics, or get involved in crusades. **One senior told me that she had subscribed to *The New York Times* once, but the papers had just piled up unread in her dorm room.** . . . Even the biological necessities get squeezed out. I was amazed to learn how little dating goes on. **Students go out in groups, and there is certainly a fair bit of partying on campus, but as one told me, "People don't have time or energy to put into real relationships."**

D. Combining in Context
Note: Compound sentences are in **boldface.**

1. Bernal Diaz, author of *The Conquest of New Spain,* entered Tenochtitlan—today's Mexico City—with Hernando Cortéz in November 1519.

   Diaz could hardly believe his eyes. **Before him there stretched a teeming metropolis of 500,000; no European city even approached that**

number. Tenochtitlan had been built over a salt marsh, and it was criss-crossed by canals. The solidly built bridges over the canals were broader than any bridges Diaz had seen; ten horsemen could easily ride abreast over them. A large, sophisticatedly engineered aqueduct carried pure water from distant springs and supplied fountains in the parks. Every kind of merchandise was on display in the marketplaces. Some of it, especially the gold and silver work, was of remarkable splendor. **Food was varied and abundant: You could buy turkeys, rabbits, deer, beans, corn, peppers, and much more.** On one side of the central square of Tenochtitlan stood the great temple of Huitzilopochtli. It was 100 feet high from its enormous base and approached by three flights of 120 steps each. **In November 1519, Cortéz himself stood in awe of the Aztec empire; within two years he had destroyed it.**

2. **Alternative medicine has become big business in the United States, and it is finally getting serious attention from medical researchers. Treatments from acupuncture to shark cartilage are being measured by the same method used for standard Western treatments: they are being tested in large studies using control groups and placebos.** This is not always simple. How do you pretend to give someone acupuncture? In one University of Maryland study, a control group received needle sticks in places where, according to traditional Chinese medicine, they should not do any good. At the University of Michigan, researchers are studying the Chinese art of qi gong, a slow-motion exercise that is said to release a healing energy. The University of Michigan study tests the benefits of qi gong for patients recovering from cardiac surgery. **One-third of the patients will be visited by a qi gong master; one-third will be visited by an imposter; one-third will receive no visits at all.** For some scientists, this research is long overdue. They believe it could add effective new therapies to current medical practice. **For others, it is a waste of money; one scientist calls such therapies "quackupuncture." Perhaps the research will demonstrate only that faith heals, but perhaps this is the most useful knowledge of all.**

Chapter 6: Relative Clauses

A. Practicing Sentence Combining

1. Children who have nowhere else to play play in the busy street.
2. I was glad to meet the woman whose cake won first prize at the fair.

3. The people who live next door have a rock band.
4. Interstate 5, which runs north and south between Canada and Mexico, was damaged in the last Los Angeles earthquake.
5. Puerto Vallarta, where I am going for my vacation, is on the Pacific Coast of Mexico.
6. Rio de Janeiro, which is the second largest city of Brazil, is known for its *Carnaval.*
7. The Middle Ages was a time when English underwent great changes.
8. *L'Avventura,* whose director, Antonioni, died in 1994, both bored and captivated its audiences.
9. Sam Shepard has called country music, whose themes are lost loves and lost lives, the only really adult music.
10. The raven, which is important in folktales and mythologies around the world, is a large completely black bird.
11. Fish wheels, which caught the salmon in buckets and dumped them out of the river, depleted the salmon runs by about 5 percent at the end of the nineteenth century.
12. Salmon canneries, which hired large numbers of Chinese workers, were very profitable for a short period of time.
13. The Chinese workers, each of whom could clean a salmon in forty-five seconds, could can a ton of salmon per hour.
14. A machine that [or *which*] worked much faster than any human could replaced the Chinese workers.
15. The machine which replaced the Chinese workers was itself soon useless.
16. Fish wheels, which are merely symptomatic of our overuse of natural resources, were finally banned in Oregon and Washington.
17. The salmon runs, which had been depleted by 50 percent before the dams were built, are now at crisis levels.
18. The salmon, which have 25 percent body fat to begin their trip up stream, enter the Columbia from the Pacific Ocean.
19. Spawning streams, in which the temperature now reaches 70°F in September, are too warm for the salmon's cold-blooded system.

20. The salmon return to their home stream where they lay their eggs and die.

C. Relative Clauses in Published Writing
From in Ian Frazier, "On the Rez," *Atlantic Monthly,* December 1999, 68; relative clauses in **boldface.**

> On another corner is the Pine Ridge post office, **which shares a large brick building with an auditorium called Billy Mills Hall,where most of the important indoor community gatherings are held.** On another corner is a two-story brick building containing tribal offices and the offices of the Oglala Department of Public Safety—the tribal police. . . . On another corner is a combination convenience store and gas station **that then was called Big Bat's Conoco and now is called Big Bat's Texaco.** Le and I parked and went in.

D. Combining in Context
Note: Relative clauses are in **boldface.**

1. The Pueblo, **who had no history of confederacy for any reason,** united briefly to drive the Spanish from their lands. When their religion was suppressed beyond their endurance, they finally began to listen to ideas of confederacy. A San Juan Pueblo medicine man named Popé was flogged and driven from San Juan Pueblo, **where the Spanish were numerous.** He went to the more distant pueblo of Taos and from there helped direct the revolt. He communicated with the other pueblos including the Hopi by sending around a piece of cloth with knots **that indicated the exact day of the revolt.** On that day, each pueblo rose, attacked, and killed the friar assigned to it and whatever Spanish soldiers and colonists **they could.** Then they moved toward Santa Fe with their Apache allies to drive out the Spanish. About 1,700 Spanish soldiers and colonists were driven out of Pueblo country and across the Rio Grande at what is today El Paso/Juarez. It was sixteen years before the Spanish recovered their position in the Pueblo area; they never reestablished control over the Hopi.
2. In 1869 John Wesley Powell, **who lost his right arm in the Civil War,** led an expedition of nine men and four boats down the Colorado River and through the Grand Canyon. For seventeen days they ran the river, gliding past hills and ledges, sweeping past sharp angles **that** [or **which**]

jutted out into the river. When they stopped briefly on a patch of dry or wet sand at the river's edge, they ate from their remaining food supply—unleavened biscuits, spoiled bacon, and lots of coffee. Then they returned to the river, **which roared constantly in their ears.** Sometimes they had difficult portages **that kept them to five miles a day.** Sometimes portage was impossible, so they stayed in the river, shooting the rapids, swirling in eddies, making thirty-five miles a day. In his journal, Powell describes the Grand Canyon as a granite prison **that** [or **which**] **in some places rose a mile above the river.** Three of the men could endure it no more and left the expedition on August 28 for an overland trip. On August 30, 1869, the remaining six men emerged from the canyon into open sky. That evening they sat around the campfire, talking of the Grand Canyon, talking of home, but talking chiefly of the three men **who had left them.** They later learned that the three men managed to climb out of the canyon but were killed by Native Americans **who mistook them for miners who had killed a Native American woman.** A couple of years after this trip, Powell made another trip down the river and turned his journals of the two trips into a book, *Explorations of the Colorado River,* **which was published in 1875.**

Chapter 7: Noun Clauses

A. Practicing Sentence Combining

1. What you spend should depend on what you earn.
2. Everybody agrees that something must be done about health care costs, but nobody agrees on how the problem should be attacked.
3. How you phrase something has everything to do with how people respond to it.
4. Analysts cannot yet predict whether the next president will be a Republican or a Democrat.
5. That she was not telling the truth emerged only after a careful piecing together of stories from many people who were intimately acquainted with the situation and the people involved.
6. Whoever leaves the room last should turn off the lights.
7. There was a time when a woman's status was determined by whom she was attached to.

8. Before making your statement, please tell us where you live, how long you have lived there, and whom you live with.
9. Some successful people are slow to admit how much of their success they owe to where they were born, when they were born, and to whom they were born.
10. It will be a long time before we can tell whether our new policy is working.
11. Some people argue about whether *Beloved* is Toni Morrison's best novel or not.
12. There is no doubt that it is an extraordinary book.
13. It concerns Sethe, a runaway slave whose house in Cincinnati is haunted by a ghost that drives off whoever comes near.
14. It soon becomes clear that the ghost is that of Sethe's daughter, Beloved.
15. Beloved materializes into a young woman who one day appears and gradually comes between Sethe and what little sanity still exists in Sethe's life.
16. She drives off Paul D., who loves Sethe but cannot understand why Sethe does whatever Beloved demands.
17. After her escape from slavery, Sethe had resolved that none of her children would ever be recaptured into slavery.
18. This determination led her into what must be called a terrible act.
19. Whether it was ultimately right or wrong is something that readers must decide for themselves.
20. How they decide may be affected by what the book teaches them about how a slave woman experienced slavery.

C. Noun Clauses in Published Writing
From Steven Pinker, *The Language Instinct* (New York: HarperPerennial, 1995), 59; noun clauses in **boldface.**

> As we shall see in this chapter, there is no scientific evidence **that languages dramatically shape their speakers' way of thinking.** But I want to do more than review the unintentionally comical history of

attempts to prove **that they do.** The idea **that language shapes thinking** seemed plausible when scientists were in the dark about **how thinking works,** or even **how we should study it.** Now that cognitive scientists know **how we should think about thinking** there is less temptation to equate it with language just because words are more palpable than thoughts. By understanding **why linguistic determinism is wrong,** we will be in a better position to understand **how language itself works** when we turn to it in the next chapters.

D. Combining in Context
Note: Noun clauses are in **boldface.**

1. **That children should be immunized against the worst childhood diseases** is accepted by most Americans today. Dramatic statistics demonstrate the success of immunization efforts in the United States. In 1934, there were approximately 2.5 million cases of whooping cough; in 1987 there were approximately 5,000. In 1952, there were approximately 21 thousand cases of polio; in 1997 there were zero. But this success is having an ironic and alarming result. Some people are beginning to wonder **whether immunizations are still necessary or desirable.** These people point to the fact **that some vaccines do cause reactions and a small number of these reactions can be severe.** However, both the risk and the consequences of a child's contracting diphtheria, tetanus, whooping cough, or polio are much greater than the risks and consequences of reaction to the vaccines. Moreover, the chance **that some disease will re-emerge as a real threat** increases with each person who does not get immunized against it. **Whether or not you vaccinate your child** can determine more than **what happens to your child.** It can determine **what happens to many other children, too. Whoever has cared for a very sick child** would not risk creating more sick children.
2. **That German could replace English as the language of the United States** seems highly unlikely today. But in the 1830s and 1840s, there were people who feared **that it could.** They pointed to the fact **that German immigrants were pouring into this country, that they were continuing to speak German among themselves, and that states had begun passing laws permitting German to be taught in public schools.** Pennsylvania and Wisconsin even permitted schools in which all instruction was in German. We should keep this in mind when we

discuss **what some people see as the current "threat" posed by Spanish in the United States.** Such people point to the large numbers of Spanish-speaking immigrants and their insistence on speaking Spanish among themselves. They also point to bilingual education. **Whether bilingual education helps or hinders immigrant children in learning English** may be debated. It may even be debated **whether bilingual education is a threat to the unity of the United States.** But those who oppose such education cannot claim **that past generations of immigrant children had to "sink or swim" in English.** Many received schooling in their native languages—languages that many of their present-day descendants do not know a word of!

Chapter 8: Adverb Clauses

A. Practicing Sentence Combining

1. If I were king, you would be queen.
2. Although some Vietnamese Americans are quite unhappy about it, the United States has moved toward diplomatic relations with Vietnam.
3. Will you love me in November as you do in May?
4. Although many Americans think of Chief Joseph as a great military leader, his role was actually to keep the men, women, and children of his band together during their attempted flight to Canada.
5. When the going gets tough, the tough get going.
6. Lord Chesterfield kept Samuel Johnson waiting a long time while Lord Chesterfield talked to someone Johnson despised.
7. Howard is the kind of person who, when you ask how he is, tells you about every ache and pain he has had in the past year.
8. If leaders surround themselves with people who are afraid to tell them the truth even at times when they are desperately wrong, they are bound to make enormous mistakes.
9. A woman needs a man as a fish needs a bicycle.[1]

---

[1] This was seen on a bumper sticker that used *like* instead of *as*. *Like* is gaining acceptability as a subordinating conjunction, but, in writing, *as* is still safer.

10. If Sergio thinks he is the only one who can do it, and if he thinks nobody else can do anything right, and if he wants to do all the work himself—then let him!
11. The witches agree among themselves to meet Macbeth when the hurlyburly is done, when the battle is lost and won.
12. After the witches plant in Macbeth's head the idea that he could be king, the idea begins to take hold of him even though it seems impossible.
13. Although Macbeth likes the idea of his being king, Lady Macbeth likes it more.
14. After they plan to murder the good, meek King Duncan, Macbeth begins to waver in his resolve as Lady Macbeth had feared he would.
15. But Lady Macbeth is as determined as Macbeth is wavering, so she takes the lead.
16. After Macbeth does the actual killing, Lady Macbeth says that she would even have done the actual killing herself if Duncan had not resembled her father as he slept.
17. Strangely, Macbeth gets stronger and crueler and Lady Macbeth gets weaker and more conscience-stricken as the play proceeds.
18. But as a voice had predicted, Macbeth sleeps no more, among other things because he is so busy killing anybody he suspects of suspecting him.
19. In Shakespeare's world, not sleeping goes against nature just as killing a king goes against nature.
20. When Macbeth says that life is "a tale / Told by an idiot, full of sound and fury / Signifying nothing," he is expressing his state of mind, not Shakespeare's view of life.

C. Adverb Clauses in Published Writing
From Timothy Ferris, *Coming of Age in the Milky Way* (New York: Anchor, 1988), 140–141; adverb clauses in **boldface.**

> **When a star runs out of fuel,** it can become unstable and explode, spewing much of its substance, now rich in iron and other heavy elements, into space. **As time passes,** this expanding bubble of gas is intermixed with passing interstellar clouds. The sun and its planets

congealed from such a cloud. Time passed, human beings appeared, miners in the north of England dug the iron from the earth, and ironmongers pounded it into nails that longshoremen loaded in barrels into the holds of H.M.S. *Endeavor.* Off the nails went to Tahiti, continuing a journey that had begun in the bowels of stars that died before the sun was born. The nails that [Captain] Cook's men traded with the Tahitian dancing girls, **while on an expedition to measure the distance of the sun,** were, themselves, the shards of ancient suns.

D. Combining in Context
Note: Adverb clauses are in **boldface.**

1. For many families, childcare is a more complicated issue today **than it was in an earlier day.** Then, many mothers stayed home with their children. Today, many mothers work outside the home. Some do it **because they have to;** others **because they want to.** Forty hours of day care per week cost about $1000 per month in Seattle in 1999. **When families can afford to pay that,** it is a matter of finding appropriate day care. **When they cannot afford it,** they must seek other solutions. Some turn to grandparents. **Although childcare by grandparents has always been a feature of life for low-income families,** it is increasingly a feature of middle-income life, too. Many families are finding that, **if they want to have children,** there must be collaboration among different branches and different generations.
2. **If you look for many turns of event in a play,** little seems to happen in Aeschylus's *Agamemnon.* Agamemnon comes home from the Trojan War and is murdered by his wife, Clytemnestra. This event springs from a number of other events that happened **before the play began.** Starting with his great-grandfather, Tantalus, Agamemnon's family history is full of parents murdering children and children murdering parents. Agamemnon himself sacrificed his daughter Iphigenia to the gods **so that he would gain their help in the Trojan War.** The play even suggests that his victories in the war involved acts of killing for which the gods will exact revenge. The play is an extended reflection on how there is no end to pain and destruction in human affairs **as long as people cling to the idea of revenge.** In the two plays that follow *Agamemnon—The Libation Bearers* (in which Agamemnon's son,

Orestes, avenges his father's death by killing his mother) and *The Eumenides*—Aeschylus shows the Greeks finally breaking the cycle of revenge. **When they do this,** they move toward civil society.

Chapter 9: Gerund Phrases

A. Practicing Sentence Combining

1. Making mistakes is often the best way to learn.
2. Learning to write should not be like crawling across a minefield under enemy fire.
3. Immediately after receiving a bomb threat, the authorities evacuated the building.
4. Opposing my country's participation in this war is not being disloyal to it.
5. When you are shopping for a bank loan, you can tell which loan costs the least by comparing annual percentage rates (APRs).
6. Valeria is known for doing what she says she will do.
7. Calling a novel religious because one of its characters is Jesus is like calling a novel scientific because one of its characters is Newton.
8. Mark's being a Nelson seems to have helped him in being promoted to top management in the Nelson Clothing Company.
9. Although the Constitution clearly makes declaring war the prerogative of the legislative branch, U.S. presidents have often gotten around this by sending military forces into action without declaring war.
10. To avoid being misled by coincidental resemblances between words from two different languages, linguists examine the evidence extremely carefully before declaring that the languages are related to a common source language.
11. Siddhartha's father tried to keep the young man's thoughts on worldly happiness by surrounding Siddhartha with unlimited luxury and pleasure.
12. Despite all their efforts, his servants could not prevent his encountering an old man, a sick man, and a corpse and realizing that living for physical pleasure is futile.

13. Siddhartha's long quest for lasting happiness led to his becoming Buddha, the Awakened One.
14. He had awakened to the knowledge that the Eightfold Path is the key to overcoming the egoistic, self-seeking desire for separate existence that is the root of human suffering.
15. If one decides to follow the path, it means adopting a rigorous program of habit formation aimed at remaking a person completely.
16. After he experienced the Great Awakening, Buddha devoted the rest of his life to preaching his message in public and counseling thousands of people in private.
17. He maintained his creativity by a regular pattern of withdrawing from the world and returning to it.
18. He made his enormous impact on people by combining extraordinary intellect and infinite compassion.
19. He resisted all attempts to turn him into a god by insisting that he was fully human.
20. His religion differed from the Hinduism of his day in being devoid of authority, ritual, speculation, and tradition.

C. Gerund Phrases in Published Writing

From Peter H. Gleick's "Harry Potter, Minus a Certain Flavour," *New York Times,* July 10, 2000, A25; gerund phrases in **boldface.**

> I am disappointed about one thing: the decision by Scholastic, publisher of the American edition, to translate the books from "English" into "American." . . . I like to think that our society would not collapse if our children started **calling their mothers Mum instead of Mom.** And I would hate to think that today's children would be frightened away from an otherwise thrilling book by **reading that the hero is wearing a jumper instead of a sweater.** . . .
>
> Do we really want children to think that crumpets are the same as English muffins? Frankly, **reading about Harry and Hermione** eating crumpets during tea is far more interesting to an American than **reading about them eating English muffins during a meal.**
>
> By **protecting our children from an occasional misunderstanding or trip to the dictionary,** we are pretending that other cultures are, or should be, the same as ours. By **insisting that everything be Americanized,** we dumb down our own society rather than enrich it.

D. Combining in Context
Note: Gerund phrases are in **boldface.**

1. Tim had asked Maria out to dinner, and this had been hard enough. **Preparing to impress her at dinner** took real research. This involved several things: **going to the restaurant in advance, getting its dinner menu to study it,** and **learning the meaning and pronunciation of all those French expressions.** That soup *du jour,* for instance. Was *jour* an animal? Maria was vegetarian, though she ate seafood. What about the eggplant *en croute?* Did that rhyme with "out" or with "hoot"? His roommate suggested just **staying away from anything with French in it.** But his roommate didn't know he had told Maria that, after **meeting her,** he was thinking of **still majoring in computer science** but **minoring in Romance languages.** He'd meant it as a joke, but she had seemed so impressed that he was stuck with it. Well, at least he was pretty sure he'd mastered the first word in *crème brûlée.*
2. For years, leaded gasoline was blamed for high atmospheric lead levels in urban areas. Authorities sought to lower these levels by **requiring that automobile engines burn unleaded gas.** New studies now suggest that the authorities should have discouraged people from **burning garbage,** which caused more pollution than **burning leaded gasoline.** Researchers examining core samples from the bottom of New York's Central Park Lake have established that the biggest rise in heavy-metal pollutants occurred between 1860 and 1930. This was before the heyday of leaded gasoline; instead, it was the heyday of incinerator construction and use in the New York area. The widespread use of leaded gasoline in the late 1960s and early 1970s added very little to the lead deposits in the lake. So maybe defenders of leaded gas were partly right when they said, "Don't knock it!"

Chapter 10: Participle Phrases

A. Practicing Sentence Combining

1. Batting the ball toward the basket, Shawn Kemp hung suspended in air.
2. Looking down the field, Steve Young found the place that Jerry Rice would reach in time to catch the ball.
3. The dirt bikes climbed the mountain trail, trailing dust, roaring in the desert air.

4. Clouds streaked across the sky, bringing rain.
5. Made from an instant mix, the espresso was extremely sweet.
6. Near the old farmhouse, the tractor sat abandoned, collecting dust, spiders, and bird nests.
7. After the picnic, Chen relaxed in the shade of the trees, listening vaguely to the conversations around him.
8. Battered and shaped by ocean winds, the trees on the Monterey Peninsula stand as sentinels on the western edge of the continent.
9. Swimming in the cool lake, feeling fish bumping against her legs, Gail made her way toward the island.
10. The cows stood in the meadow, munching grass, mooing occasionally.
11. Ordered to their seats, the children reluctantly stopped watching the commotion in the hall.
12. Like giant insects, the combines moved across the grain-covered hills, cutting the wheat in broad swaths.
13. The salmon swim upstream against the water flow, leaping fifteen-foot waterfalls.
14. The dams, built to supply water to irrigate desert land and to supply hydroelectric power, stop the salmon.
15. After the sunny weather, the seeds begin to sprout, poking the dirt up in miniature ridges.
16. Nearing the top of the mountain, the hiker stepped dangerously near the edge.
17. Carved by thousands of years of wind and snow and rain, the edge scooped back, dropping a thousand feet to the valley below.
18. Looking at the breathtaking view, the hiker fell to her knees.
19. Whistling around her ears, the wind drowned out the sound of her own heartbeat.
20. Returning to her car, the hiker was aware that she had had a transforming experience.

B. Catching the Dangling Modifier

1. Wanting only peace and quiet, I heard the bus roar down the street.
2. I stood on the corner, shifting from foot to foot. Finally, the light changed.

3. We had not eaten since breakfast; finally, dinner arrived just before we began eating the salt in the salt shaker.
4. Grounded for two months by her father, she was filled with anger.
5. Searching through the wreckage left by the earthquake, the rescuers found a four-year-old boy.

D. Participle Phrases in Published Writing
From Diane Ackerman, *The Moon by Whale Light and Other Adventures among Bats, Penguins, Crocodilians, and Whales* (New York: Random House, 1991), 6; participle phrases in **boldface.**

> A hawk appeared, swooped, grabbed a bat straight out of the sky, and disappeared with it. In a moment, the hawk returned, but **hearing his wings coming,** the bats all shifted sideways to confuse him, and he missed. As wave upon wave of bats poured out of the cave, their collective wings began to sound like drizzle on autumn leaves. **Gushing out and swirling fast in this living Mixmaster,** newly risen bats started in close and then veered out almost to the rim of the bowl, **climbing until they were high enough to clear the ridge.** Already, a long black column of bats looked like a tornado **spinning out far across the Texas sky.** A second column formed, **undulating and dancing through the air like a Chinese dragon, stretching for miles, headed for some unknown feeding ground.** The night was silent except for the serene beating of their wings.

E. Combining in Context
Note: Participle phrases are in **boldface.**

1. Lewis and Clark readied themselves for the trip down the Snake and the Columbia, **making arrangements to leave their horses with the Nez Perce, hiring two guides, making dugout canoes.** On October 16, 1805, they entered the Columbia. **Passing a burial ground,** they decided to stop. **Looking briefly at the human bones and wrapped bodies on the burial platform and at the horse bones around the platform,** they pushed on. Along the river were numerous Native American lodges and Native Americans **splitting and drying the abundant salmon.** Lewis and Clark traded trinkets for salmon, roots, and dog, the latter **being the favorite food of the expedition. Nearing the big falls of the Columbia,** they found the water **getting more and more**

turbulent. At what is today called The Dalles, they had to portage all their food and equipment and lower the boats with lines along the southern edge. One boat got away when the line broke, **causing much excitement among the Native Americans watching and helping the expedition.** Once they were below the falls, they found bigger, flatter, and highly decorated ocean-going canoes. They were near their goal, the mouth of the Columbia.

2. One night at Yosemite John Muir watched the moon on a waterfall. At midnight, the moonlight made a rainbow 500 feet below where Muir stood. **Deciding to get behind the waterfall and watch the moonlight coming through the water,** Muir stepped out onto the rocky ledge, **making his way along a ridge** that was only six inches wide in one place. Suddenly the wind shifted, **sending water pounding down on Muir's head and shoulders. Kneeling down,** Muir waited for a chance to move farther back under the falls. He found a rock and a chunk of ice to wedge himself in. Finally the wind shifted again. **Dashing for freedom,** Muir escaped the ledge and made a fire to warm his numb limbs.

Chapter 11: Infinitive Phrases

A. Practicing Sentence Combining

1. She went to the suburbs to find cheap fencing.
   or
   To find cheap fencing, she went to the suburbs.
2. Gerrard hoped to find a cure for prostate cancer.
3. Andre expected to win the Boston Marathon and to become an Olympic Medal winner.
4. To have John involved meant tension and anxiety.
5. In the nineteenth century, doctors made a decision to remove women's wombs to cure their hysteria.
6. The bride had done innumerable hours of physical therapy to walk down the aisle at her wedding.
7. To grow orchids in one's house requires no special talent.
8. To work with our dreams is to be in touch with our deepest truths.
9. Alex climbed Mt. Rainier to celebrate her fortieth birthday.

10. Ruby hung her clothes on the clothesline for the wind to fluff them and the sun to dry them.
11. Frank Chin and Jeffery Paul Chan expected to create an anthology of Asian American writing.
12. They contacted Lawson Inada and Shawn Wong to find help with their project.
13. The four of them did extensive research to find the earliest examples of Chinese and Japanese American writing.
14. They even found a way to include writing from the detention cells on Angel Island in San Francisco Bay.
15. They traveled to California to talk with John Okada's widow.
16. They chose the name *Aiiieeeee* to scorn the only word that American comics had allowed Asian Americans to say.
17. There was no reason to believe that *Aiiieeeee* would be a success or to believe that Americans were ready to read the works of Asian Americans.
18. Because *Aiiieeeee* was successful, they decided to do another anthology to be called *The Big Aiiieeeee.*
19. Since the publication of *The Big Aiiieeeee,* there is a need to find a place where new Asian American writers can be published.
20. Now Vietnamese, Koreans, and Cambodians have a desire to be heard as Americans.

C. Infinitive Phrases in Published Writing
From Harold Kushner, *When All You've Ever Wanted Isn't Enough* (New York: Pocket Books, 1986), 91; infinitive phrases in **boldface.**

> My dinner companion was telling me that the way **to get through a life of tragedy and uncertainty** was **to accept it and yield to it,** rather than **fight it,** like an Oriental wrestler using his opponent's weight and strength against him rather than trying **to meet him head-on.** But he also tried **to tell me** that the way **to keep from going through life in constant pain** was **to lower your expectations.** Do not expect **life to be fair,** and you will not have your heart broken by injustice. There have always been crime, corruption, and accidents, and there always will be. It is part of the human condition.

(A teacher of mine used to say, "Expecting **the world to treat you fairly** because you are a good person is like expecting **the bull not to charge because you are a vegetarian."**)

D. Combining in Context

1. Builders are finding economical ways **to use recycled items in their building.** Recycled items have been available for several years, but in the past, the decision **to use them** was a decision **to spend extra money.** Now it is actually cheaper **to use some recycled and reclaimed items** than **to use new items.** Topsoil, concrete, and steel are being reclaimed and reused rather than being sent to a landfill. Old paint turned in to household hazardous waste sites is mixed and recolored and used in public buildings. Concrete floor tiles are made from ground Mexican glass beer bottles. Even old carpet is being recycled. It is actually cheaper **to clean the carpet thoroughly,** then **retexturize it,** and **add designs and colors** than **to put it in a landfill** and **buy new carpet.** A public building in Seattle, the city known for it rainy weather, is practicing an ongoing form of recycling. It is collecting rainwater **to use to flush toilets.**
2. When people who speak different languages meet frequently **to trade,** they need some way **to communicate with one another.** The same need arises in the colonization of another country or in workplaces where the workers (including slaves) may speak different languages from one another and from the boss. The language that is created in such situations is called a pidgin. Pidgins are made up of words from the languages of the contributing groups, but one language often contributes more than the others. In order **to be pronounceable by all speakers,** a pidgin cannot have sounds that are not present in all the contributing languages. In addition to this limitation in sounds, there is a very limited vocabulary, a vocabulary of nouns, verbs, and adjectives. The words also usually have specific referents in the tangible world. Pidgin is a language that is used **to get a job done.** Pidgins also lack clear syntax, with different people and even the same people arranging words differently when they mean the same thing. There are almost no purely structural words such as conjunctions and prepositions. Some pidgins remain pidgins forever or die out when the need for them disappears. Russonorsk is an example of such a pidgin. It was spoken in the nineteenth century by adult Russian and Norwegian fishermen **to**

transact business when they met together for brief visits in the Arctic. The speakers of this pidgin continued **to speak their native languages** when they communicated at home and in their home country.

But sometimes a pidgin gets spoken at home, and it takes the place of a native language for couples who do not speak one another's language. The children in this home need a language **to express feelings and complex ideas;** they need more words than those with tangible referents. And so within a couple of generations a creole is born. It seems that there is a natural language-making part of the brain that creates language when none is available. People need languages **to express the complexities of human experience,** and the language-making part of the brain is there **to help fulfill that need.** Eventually creoles evolve into full-fledged languages with even larger vocabularies and complex grammars if the need is there.

Chapter 12: Nominative Absolute Phrases

A. Practicing Sentence Combining

1. In Andrew Wyeth's painting *Christina's World,* Christina kneels in the foreground, her hands grasping the dried grass.
   or
   In Andrew Wyeth's painting *Christina's World,* Christina, her hands grasping the dried grass, kneels in the foreground.
2. The bus roared down the street, its passengers grabbing for something to hang on to.
   or
   Its passengers grabbing for something to hang on to, the bus roared down the street.
3. The government offices were closed for an hour, their flags at half-mast.
4. The lake shimmered in the moonlight, its clear surface cool and inviting.
   or
   Its clear surface cool and inviting, the lake shimmered in the moonlight.
5. The lights out, the audience suddenly became silent.
6. Doan sat in the chair, his sprained ankle resting on the stool in front of him.

7. Katerina skated away, the blades of her skates reflecting the colored lights of the arena.
   or
   The blades of her skates reflecting the colored lights of the arena, Katerina skated away.
8. Mark Spitz emerged from the water, his perfect dive completed.
9. Their teeth straightened, their mouths smiling, middle-class American children face the future with confidence.
10. Her body emaciated, her self-esteem destroyed, the model entered the Betty Ford Clinic.
    or
    The model entered the Betty Ford Clinic, her body emaciated, her self-esteem destroyed.
11. The Zuni *lhamanas* bridged two genders, their physiology male, their dress female, their cultural roles both male and female.
    or
    Their physiology male, their dress female, their cultural roles both male and female, the Zuni *lhamanas* bridged two genders.
12. Their clothes needing washing, the missionaries looked for a Zuni to do their laundry.
13. His roles flexible, the *lhamana,* Wé Wha, was the only one in the pueblo who would do the laundry of outsiders.
14. Their religion finding any deviation from two separate and distinct sexes sinful, the missionaries were outraged.
15. His hair combed like a woman's, his dress the clothing of a woman, Wé Wha was taken for a woman in Washington D.C.
16. The anthropologist Mrs. Stevenson having many male characteristics, Wé Wha seems to have considered her similar to himself.
17. Face covered with the mask of the *Kolhamana* kachina, the *lhamana* played the role of the *lhamana* kachina in various ceremonies.
    or
    The *lhamana* played the role of the *lhamana* kachina in various ceremonies, his face covered with the mask of the *Kolhamana* kachina.
18. Today *berdache* is the word used by anthropologists to refer to Zuni *lhamanas* and to people fulfilling a similar role in other Native American

tribes, most Native American tribes in South, Central, and North America having a special place inside the community for third-gender people.

19. Knowledge of the history of the *berdache* in pre-Columbian America being restored to them, gay Native Americans have a new idea of their place in tribal life.
20. Gender designators of clothing and role in the community defining the *berdache, berdache* cannot be translated as "gay" or "homosexual," terms referring only to sexual orientation in Western culture.

C. Nominative Absolute Phrases in Published Writing
From Gregory Martin, *Mountain City* (New York: North Point Press, 2000), 14; nominative absolute phrases in **boldface.**

> Then all them Boscos would show at the Overland in their funeral clothes and Aita would herd 'em into the recyvydor and the deceased would be laid out in a suit in a casket in the middle of the room. (Aita kept the suit and the casket in the closet.) We might have fifty Boscos corralled in there. Ama would say a prayer and we'd all bow our heads and Aita would take a picture of everyone gathered around the open casket looking serious, **the men with their hands behind their backs, the women fingering rosaries.** And not long after, everybody'd go back to where they were before. Aita would send the photograph and a note to the family back in the old country.

D. Combining in Context
Note: Nominative absolute phrases are in **boldface.**

1. In the mid-October chill, the tomatoes still hang on the vines, **their peach and pale green tones aiming toward ripeness.** The nights are getting too cold, the days too short for me to hope that they will ripen here in the garden on the vine. If I leave them, they will succumb to slugs and split skins, and all manner of rot and decay. So I pick them, dozens of them, and bring them in to ripen. I try every method I know to bring them to ripe redness—brown paper bags, individual newspaper wrap, sitting in the open air on my counter. A few will make it, **their skin deep red, their tomato smell and sweet acidy flavor bringing August into my late October kitchen.**

2. Snow is late in Colorado this year. The skiers are sitting at home in shorts and T-shirts, **their skis waxed, their gear packed, ready for fun.** But La Niña keeps the weather warm and dry. Soon, however, the snows must come. A low pressure system from the west will meet a cold front from the north, and winter will arrive. The first big storm of the year will blanket the mountains in white, and the season will begin.

Chapter 13: Coordination, Parallelism, and Balance

A. Practicing Sentence Combining

1. Benjamin got as far as he got by being hardworking, thrifty, and, above all, honest.
2. Shakespeare's history plays show that the qualities that make a good king may be different from the qualities that make a good person.
3. Our conversation last night went a long way toward resolving some of our differences, improving communication between us, and making our whole future together look brighter.
4. Patriotism consists not only of waving your country's flag but also of attempting to correct your country's faults.
5. At the beginning of the year, they were inseparable lovers; at the end of the year, they were bitter enemies.
6. Couples were everywhere, whirling around the dance floor in the ballroom, whispering in the corners of the terrace, wandering into the shadows of the deep gardens beyond.
7. He thought he was cheating the system, but he was really cheating himself.
8. The digestive process begins in the mouth, continues in the stomach, and is completed in the intestines.
9. As Martin Luther King Jr. pointed out, freedom is not usually given to the oppressed, but taken from the oppressor.
10. If you want to use it to its full capacity, a home computer can keep track of your finances, become a whole shopping center at your fingertips, turn on your coffeemaker at different times on different mornings, read the weather report and decide whether to run the sprinkler system, run your alarm system, remind you that your mother's birthday is coming, and even supply you with rhyming words if you make up your own poem about how much she means to you.

11. Some people consider multiculturalism a dangerous trend in the United States; others consider it an important goal, and still others consider it a simple fact.
12. That we are now a nation of many cultures, religions, and ethnic identities seems beyond question.
13. Until recently, the nation thought of itself as a melting pot that people went into Italian or German or Russian Jewish and came out American.
14. Because this American identity was essentially white European in origin, the melting pot worked somewhat well for European immigrant groups with white skin, but less well for others.
15. People of non-European ethnicity or skin color were often excluded from the melting pot by laws, business practices, and social prejudice.
16. Even those who could assimilate did so at the price of giving up their own cultural practices and never seeing their experiences and contributions reflected in the country's history books.
17. This has led some people to call for the replacement of the melting pot with the salad bowl, in which ingredients retain their identities while making their distinctive contributions to the flavor of the whole.
18. Others worry that it is not possible to have cultural diversity and national unity at the same time.
19. Multiculturalists answer that it is a matter not of possibility but of necessity.
20. It is also, in their view, a glorious opportunity to achieve a nation even richer, stronger, and more beautiful than we already have.

C. Coordination, Parallelism, and Balance in Published Writing
From Jared Diamond, *Guns, Germs, and Steel: The Fates of Human Societies* (New York: W. W. Norton, 1997), 284; coordination, parallelism, and balance in **boldface.**

> We have seen that **large or dense** populations arise only **under conditions of food production, or at least under exceptionally productive conditions for hunting-gathering. Some productive hunter-gatherer societies reached the organizational level of chiefdoms, but none reached the level of states;** all states nourish their citizens by food production. These considerations, along with the just

mentioned correlation between **regional population size and societal complexity,** have led to a protracted chicken-or-egg debate about the causal relations **between food production, population variable, and societal complexity.** Is it intensive food production that is the cause, **triggering population growth and somehow leading to a complex society**? Or are **large populations and complex societies instead the cause, somehow leading to intensification of food production**?

D. Combining in Context

1. Although **she was in love with at least two men during her life and her councilors and Parliament pushed her to marry,** Elizabeth I had many reasons to remain a virgin queen. **One was that she did not want to be ruled by a man;** the rules of marriage at that time dictated that a married woman was ruled by her husband. **Another reason was that she was concerned about succession.** If Elizabeth had a son, there would be many in England and in the rest of Europe who would be drawn to a rebellion around her son, a male ruler. **Fear of dying in childbirth might have been another reason.** It was certainly not uncommon for a young healthy woman to die in childbirth in medieval times. **And finally, by not marrying, Elizabeth could fashion herself the Virgin Queen, a Protestant replacement for the Virgin Mary.** Elizabeth had herself dethroned the Virgin Mary when, as a Protestant, she succeeded her Catholic half-sister. As the Virgin Queen, she could be married only to the people of England and thus claim their **adoration and loyalty.**
2. On Memorial Day, **Mom will come, and Grandma will come, and aunts and uncles will come. They will come, flowers and hoes and rakes in hand,** in a procession up the hill to your corner. **They will come chattering of the flowers on Uncle Dan's grave, the weeds on Aunt Adeline's, the new curb around Conrad's plot, the plastic flowers Bucks always bring, the Wolfrums, who never come at all. They will pull the weeds from your plot, they will pour water over your stone to wash off the dust of spring plowing, they will rake the sand into straight lines. They will leave peonies and lilacs and coral bells in a foil-covered can over your bones and lay a yellow rose on your tombstone.** Do they hear the silence into which the meadowlark sings?

Index

Note: Glossary pages appear in italics.